SELF-VALUE:
THE STORY OF ME

"An Autobiography by"

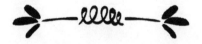

Brandon Williams

Table of Contents

Introduction

During my adolescent years I was exposed to and experienced many hardships. I've counseled men and women on many of those ills such as domestic violence, drug abuse, depression, homelessness, and on practicing self-value. As a public speaker, one frequent message I've conveyed is real love shouldn't hurt. This causes my audience to question if the love they receive hurts them emotionally or physically.

I am a by-product of all that is least desired and overlooked. When I was seven, I was functioning as an adult. By the time I made twelve, I was on my own and raised myself from that time forward. I grew up in a low-income community and was homeless most of my childhood. I've sold various illegal drugs, generally crack cocaine. I routinely engaged in a wide range of criminal activities primarily burglaries, robberies, possessing illegal guns, attempted murder and conspiracy to commit murder. I never knew my father therefore my mother was faced with the task of mastering both the roles of being mother and father. I witnessed my mother suffer many unforgiving attacks by her longtime crack addict boyfriend. Revisiting moments like these has been troubling, but I've found healing in sharing my story. I also established

by Brandon Williams

it's curing to the hearts and minds of the readers who has or is currently living in similar situations. I humbly and graciously accept my purpose in life as one who strengthens the nation and gives voice to the voiceless.

My life story is about a mother and son in peril that finds serenity through their faith. In sharing my story, I highlight many problems society is faced with today such as domestic violence, illiteracy, bullying, low self-esteem, depression, and suicide. My story resonates with people fighting against those conditions and similar life experiences. This account of grand proportion has its fair share of humor, inspiration, suspense, betrayal, crime, sex and romance. Self-Value: The Story of Me, is an eye-opening, poignant, often hilarious story that explores my twelve years of childhood homelessness, juvenile delinquency and success. The story begins with Brandon, a seven-year-old boy witnessing his mother and her abusive boyfriend huffing crack vapors from a coke can, a makeshift crack pipe, at their kitchen table in 1988. During the time the crack epidemic exploded within the black community. Each chapter in Self-Value: The Story of Me can stand alone. They chronicle the storyline of my childhood and adolescent experiences, over a decade of crime; crack and marijuana dealing, attempted murder, conspiracy to commit murder, burglaries, robberies, and suicidal acts. The stories are arranged like a crazy quilt of turmoil in all their awe-inspiring, often dramatic and occasionally fear-provoking individuality. I believe that practicing self-value can lead to life improvement. Self-Value is a theme within my book. Self-

Value is being audacious enough to constantly love and realize the value in yourself, even when no one else does. Given guidance and support, at-risk youth and impoverished families will find their own best way to live a productive life.

I've laughed and cried with countless free and incarcerated young men and women. I've listened to their stories. I've watched them steal, paint the inner-city streets crimson red with innocent blood, struggle with depression and self-destruct. I've arrested many of these youth and their parents, but I've counseled more. Nothing in my urban upbringing in the Deep South prepared me for the journey that practicing self-value has brought me. There are many books today that are geared towards urban youth and inner-city families, very few of those books have been written by one.

In this book the reader will experience my life as a police officer. I am a former police officer, with over a decade of die-hard and engaging experiences. I've witnessed, experienced and fought against many unsettling occurrences of police brutality and racial profiling. I've since founded and run a nonprofit that raises awareness in underserved communities and provides aid to reduce juvenile delinquency. This book offers an inside, behind the scene perspective on the aforementioned topics. Besides this, I am from the inner city and have been blessed to overcome many of the struggles that suppress today's youth. Since I was a small child, I dreamed of sharing my story because

by Brandon Williams

I realized my life wasn't normal. My life story reads like a movie script filled with comedy, drama and tragedy.

Addiction and Abuse

People often say, "Life isn't a bed of roses," but I later discovered in it lays the seeds, soil and all other fundamentals required to build one.

I was awake. My brother would not stop wiggling in his sleep and now I was roused. As I lay there in the twilight of sleep and wakefulness, I turned my head slightly and looked into the kitchen where the light was still on. What I saw astounded and confused me. I moved my body softly and carefully, lifting myself up a little bit from the twin bed where we were sleeping to get a better view. The kitchen was adjacent to the head of our little bed, located in the living room, and I did not want my mother—and certainly not her abusive boyfriend—to hear me. I could not help myself, though, because they were doing the strangest thing. They had a crumpled Coke can and were passing it back and forth between them. But, obviously, this can was not filled with its normal, bubbly Coca-Cola drink. I could tell that much because they were holding the can horizontally and lighting a cigarette lighter on top of it. I watched wide-eyed as my mother sat calmly at the kitchen table and held the crumpled-up coke can to her mouth, inhaling the smoke

5

and fumes wafting out of the holes punctured in the side. I did not know what it was, and I did not know what she was doing, but I will never forget the night I witnessed this scene. I quietly woke my brother and asked him to take a look. We both lay there, staring into the kitchen with utter amazement.

It was not too much later that I learned they were putting crack cocaine on top of that Coke can, dissolving it with the flame and using it as a crack pipe. That evening was the first time I had witnessed my mother smoke crack. Unfortunately, it was not the last time.

I had gone to bed that evening in a stable state of mind. After a while, I laid my head back down and eventually fell asleep, but it was a pretty hard scene to understand at such a young age. The next day, I was awoken to a very unstable childhood. Everything I knew about my world changed from that point forward. I never spoke of that moment for weeks. As an adult, my heart breaks when I think back to this moment in time when I was an innocent seven-year-old boy and my eyes were opened.

The memories of my childhood that replay themselves in my head are vivid, almost like looking back into my past through a window. As I write, it makes me sad this very moment. Crack has been an epidemic that has plagued the African-American community and other urban minorities since its induction into America's drug market. Crack, to most families, means loss in every facet of the word. Everything that you love and hope for diminishes as you watch helplessly as crack takes over your life. Something as simple as going to the store and buying groceries will become difficult for most families. Crack has killed more black people than the Ku Klux Klan, the AIDS epidemic and black-on-black crime combined. Crack is the cancer of the black family. Just like cancer eats away the bone marrow of the human body, crack eats away the structure and foundation of the black family. From birth until the age of seven, my life was what I would consider "normal". Things felt perfect: I got Christmas gifts for Christmas, birthday gifts on my birthday, and new school clothes when I needed them. I got help with homework assignments when I needed assistance. My mother bought me lots of toys; I had a new action figure whenever a new one came out. I enjoyed eating to my stomach's satisfaction. Yes, I witnessed my mother and her boyfriend having fights and arguments, but this was part of my normal life, too. I was happy, and I could not imagine anything better. Then my mother was introduced to a new friend: crack cocaine. Consequently, the things I loved and enjoyed as a kid abruptly came to an end.

Because of my mother's addiction to crack, we were also subject to the same effects and backlashes of the crack epidemic as any other family. She and her boyfriend's constant arguments began to escalate into fights—ones that usually ended with outcries from my mother pleading for him to stop. For the record, my mother was not a pushover at all. In fact, despite being physically weaker than her boyfriend, she fought back and held her own with just cause. A lot of their fights and arguments were amplified and became more violent once their drug addiction was added to the equation. Following these fights, my mother's boyfriend would usually pack his belongings and leave for the night.

The next day, I would go to school feeling overwhelmed with shame because I feared that my classmates would find out about my mother's drug addiction. Although I believed my peers were well aware, no one ever confronted me about it. The constant fear of being embarrassed by the affairs of my family life caused me to grow distant from my friends. This was my way of ensuring that no one would ever find out. Nevertheless, this method of insulating and protecting myself evolved into me being diagnosed with an antisocial disorder.

My mother was cool, vibrant and quite the looker, as well. Gregory was a very jealous and controlling man. His own insecurities and afflictions warranted the merciless beatings my mother suffered by his hands. After battering her dearly, Gregory would come back the next day begging for her forgiveness, and she would forgive him. As a child, I would study my mother's bruised face, her blackened eyes and the bruises on her neck. As I did, I would also wonder what she did to merit such brutality. With bright beaming eyes and a grin on her face, she still insists that she is just as beautiful today as she was nearly two decades ago. "Yes, Mother, you still 'have it'," I assured her, with a less than certain tone of voice as I laughed faintly.

From the beginning, Gregory and my mother enjoyed drinking wine and playing card games with their friends, preferring Spades or Tonk. I always enjoyed their playfulness and camaraderie when they would gather together around the old wooden table, drinking and playing cards for hours. "You reneged, now give me my damn books," someone would occasionally yell. This was an indicator that the other person or team had failed to play the correct suit of cards.

One evening in particular, I watched as my mother tallied up the score on a scratch sheet of paper, taking one final puff of her cigarette before flinging it away. "That's Game," she announced to the table.

An opposing team member grabbed the sheet of paper my mother had been scribbling on for the past hour, looked it over thoroughly and nodded his head. "Yeah... Yeah, that's game," he assured his frustrated teammate.

The card game ended and the crowd around the table systematically disbursed. The evening was over. My brother and I were already in bed. My mother and Gregory went into their bedroom. All was quiet. Mischievously, I slipped out of bed, snuck into the kitchen and sipped away the remaining corner of Mad Dog 20/20 that was left on the table. A cheap wine that comes in various fruity flavors, Mad Dog 20/20 is beloved by winos who know they can get inebriated quickly by the stuff. It also helps that it has a mild scent and can be passed off as juice or soda when poured in the right container.

Suddenly, I heard yelling from my mother's bedroom. I anxiously threw the bottle of wine down and ran back into the living room, so they would not find me in the kitchen drinking it. Seconds later, I heard a loud thump and then another. I slipped into bed, my mouth a bit numb and my stomach welling with the warmth of the alcohol. Their bedroom walls vibrated, and I curled up next to my brother, holding my breath. Then, I heard the sound of wall fixtures crashing onto the floor. Gregory was shouting viciously at my mother. *Mother!* I leapt out of bed and ran to the bedroom. The door was shut, so I cautiously turned the knob and cracked it open. I could see my mother lying on the floor, lifeless but still gasping for air. Gregory had straddled himself across my mother's lap and was clenching her neck with both hands, choking her as she struggled to gasp for air. Gregory's shirt was drenched in sweat and he seemed to be exhausted from the prolonged beating he had inflicted upon my mother. The sweat on his hands caused his grip around Mother's neck to loosen and I hoped he would give up. To my horror, he readjusted his merciless hands to apply more pressure.

"Stop! Stop!...Stop! Please don't kill her! Please don't kill my mother!" I yelled to him.

He seemed to hear me because he released his grip. But then he slapped her face. I was screaming for him to stop. He proceeded to strike her several times in the face, knocking her head backwards into the wall each time he punched her. I screamed louder and louder for him to stop. He finally got up and started packing some of his clothing, cursing and yelling at the top of his lungs.

Wiping away the blood from her nose, neck area and mouth with a blanket, my mother told me to go back into the living room. I stood there, paralyzed. As she was getting up from the floor, Gregory stalked back over to her and choked her again, slamming her into the wall. She collapsed to the floor next to some shattered glass from a picture frame that had fallen off the wall. Gregory strode out of the bedroom, through the living room and left through the front door. Thinking quickly, I ran to the front door and locked it. I returned and found my mother in the bathroom cleaning up. I watched her in silence, stunned.

After she cleaned her wounds, she went back into the bedroom and started picking up overturned furniture. I asked why he did this to her, but she did not answer. My mother and I sat in the living room quietly and watched television until I fell asleep. The next morning, she woke me up, so I could get prepared for school. I went into the bathroom and got into the shower. I got dressed and grabbed my book sack. As I was walking out the door, I kissed my mother and said, "I love you."

by Brandon Williams

I sat in class the entire day, replaying the graphic and horrific images witnessed the night before. My teacher kept calling me. "Brandon, are you okay? Son, you have to pay attention!"

I kept to myself, silently trying to understand what had happened. Finally, the school bell rang, and class was dismissed for the day. I was not sure if I felt relieved or anxious to go home. As I walked outside to board the school bus, I was surprised to hear my mother's voice calling for me.

"Here, Brandon... Here! Over here!" she motioned with her hands as I traced the sound of her voice. She was leaning against Madea's car wearing a dark pair of shades with her hair draped over her face. As I got closer, I could see my uncle Andrew in the driver's seat and my Grandmother Natalie, "Madea", seated in the rear passenger seat. When my mother explained that we were going to live with Madea for a while, until we found a home of our own, I smiled for the first time that day. I got into the car and we drove back home. My brother Charles was just getting off the school bus a few blocks away when we arrived. We went inside and started packing our clothing and whatever else my mother could fit into Madea's 1977 Chevy Nova.

With the rear end of the car scraping the ground from overpacking, we drove away. I was eager to see what the future had in store for us as we embarked on a new journey. Madea gave us a room to share in her house and we unpacked all of our belongings in there.

After only a few days of living with Madea, however, she began to demand money from my mother. Madea was very obsessed with the idea of being paid for anything she did for my mother. Mother agreed and started giving her a substantial portion of the welfare check she received for us. My mother also gave Madea most of the food stamps she received, as well. After a few weeks had passed, Madea demanded that my mother hand over her entire welfare check and the whole sum of food stamps that she was awarded. My mother told Madea that her request was unreasonable and refused. Madea then threatened to throw us out of the house. I was scared because we would not have anywhere to stay if she did.

During this time, my mother began to speak more frequently with Gregory. Madea became hardnosed in order to control my mother, and she continued to abuse us verbally. She forced my mother to move out. Consequently, she reconciled with Gregory. Soon after, we were back to square one, living with this abusive man for a second time. And mother's drug addiction disrupted our lives even more than ever. Soon, we found ourselves constantly needing food and having our lights turned off more frequently. Gregory continued to beat my mother whenever he got upset about something. My mother being tossed about and thrown throughout the house was a sight I could never grow accustomed to seeing. I remember Charles jumping into one of Gregory's attacks, trying to protect her. Needless to say, he was not successful. Charles was one year older than me, but a lot smaller. But I must say that he was a lot more courageous than I was at that time. I was merely a "momma's boy". I was timid and shy, but I was also quick to run and tattle on anyone who did something I did not like.

Mother and Gregory continued to get behind on rent payments and we lost our home. My mother spoke to our cousin, Rhonda Hayward, and asked if we could live in a vacant home she owned in town. Without hesitation, Rhonda agreed and told us we could live there rent-free. The house was beautiful, and we were very proud of it. For a moment, I began to feel like hope was siding with us for a change.

But to my dismay, having a new home did not stop the hunger and craving for crack that saturated the minds of my mother and her boyfriend. The arguments and the fights continued, as did the occult-like lifestyle of my mother's addiction to crack cocaine. Nearly a year had passed since the night I witnessed my mother smoke crack. I was not so innocent anymore. I knew what caused that Coke can to puff out smoke now.

My heart still harbored the piercing fear that, someday, my peers might find out about my life outside of school. I was never content with myself or my family. I was ashamed and very embarrassed about my life. These are insecurities which I carried with me throughout my childhood. Life was very challenging, and I could not quite grasp or fully understand why my life was so chaotic.

Gregory and Mother conceived a child. A baby girl! In late April of 1989, my little sister Jessica, "Jess", was born and this caused my mother to stay home a lot more. Charles and I were happy to have a little sister. Even this ray of hope, though, could not quell my mother's craving to be in the street searching for another "hit" of crack. My mother and Gregory would leave us at home with our sister, so they could go smoke crack. Dilated pupils and the smell of burnt plastic was an indicator that their search was successful. Gregory continued to verbally and physically abuse her, and two years later, my mother gave birth to my baby brother, Derrick. Several months after Derrick was born, my mother became pregnant for a third time and separated from Gregory. He and his sister were trying to gain custody of Jess. He did not attempt to gain custody of Derrick because it was rumored that he was not the father. Gregory and his sister tried to capitalize on the fact that my mother was a drug addict as grounds for her to lose custody. Yes, Gregory was still a crack addict, too. But his sister was unable to have children. He wanted his barren sister to be awarded custody of Jess on his behalf. Mother feared that if they took her to court, they might win the case, so she asked Madea to take temporary custody of us. Once she explained to Madea that she would give her all of the food stamps and welfare money that the government awarded us, Madea agreed.

I recall my mother telling me about an incident where she was walking through the town of Glendale with Jess. She told me that

Gregory was riding in a car with his sister and happened to see her. He jumped out of the vehicle and snatched Jess out of her arms. My mother told me that she ran behind the car, trying to catch it as they drove off. My mother said that she later found them in the District Attorney's office pleading for custody of Jess. The D.A. told Gregory and his sister to give Jess back to her.

After that ordeal, Mother and Gregory unbelievably reconciled their differences and got back together. She sold drugs for drug dealers in exchange for crack, which she and Gregory would smoke. Gregory worked a steady job and most of his earnings were spent on crack, as was the welfare check the government granted my mother for me and my siblings. A great portion of our food stamps was sold in exchange for cash and the monies gained were invested to support their addiction, as well. In the street, a hundred dollars in food stamps are worth fifty in cash. If we had three hundred dollars in food stamps, someone would offer to buy them for only one hundred and fifty dollars. My youngest sister Meagan, "Star", wasn't born until the summer of 1992. It was unfortunate for my younger siblings, at that time, because they never experienced the memorable moments that Charles and I shared with our mother years before she became an addict. They never saw the strong, God-fearing woman that sat down with us night after night, reading passages from the Bible and other related materials. The application of Biblical teachings and being godly people were my mother's precepts. All my younger siblings ever knew, though, were the negative effects crack had on their lives: Poverty and frustration.

Then, my mother was arrested for a probation violation on an earlier conviction in 1988 for Grand Theft Auto. At this point, my siblings and I were placed in the court's care. We became "Wards of the Court", which meant the judicial system assumed full rights and had legal custody of us. My mother wrote the judge a letter requesting that we be placed with our grandmother. She feared that if we went to a foster home, we would be split up and it would be very difficult for her to get us back. The judge agreed to grant custody to our grandmother, and Madea became our legal guardian.

I continued to go to school concealing, to the best of my ability, all of the afflictions of my life at home. I was withdrawn. I never really cared about what was going on at school or with my peers. I did not have an interest in learning. The only thing I can honestly recall from my time in elementary school is writing horror stories and dreaming of one day becoming a scientist. At the end of my fourth-grade year, I received the devastating news that I would be retained. I felt humiliated repeating the fourth grade. I just could not get things into perspective. I could not focus on school because my home life dominated my thoughts.

So, the following year, I repeated the fourth grade again.

Searching for Peace

We were happy to remain together as a family and knew that we were unlike most families that were wards of the court. When my grandmother, Madea, took custody of the four of us, I was eleven years old, my brother Charles was twelve, my sister Jess was three and my little brother Derrick was one. In addition, my Mother was pregnant with my youngest sister, Star. I knew my grandmother fairly well; I had always perceived her as being a very sweet and polite woman. But those preconceived notions quickly diminished after we moved in with her. My mother sat me down one day and explained that my grandmother was mentally unstable and suffered from numerous mental illnesses. My grandmother's father was a white man that she knew little about. As a young girl, my grandmother was attacked and raped repeatedly by familiar faces. My mother believed that my grandmother's childhood was part of the reason why she was mentally unstable. Learning of this story saddened me, and it made me very forgiving towards her. Later on in life, I had the opportunity to sit down one-on-one with my grandmother and she told me her personal account of what she had experienced. From the very first day of moving into my grandmother's home, we had a troubled relationship. I quickly found that when the entire family gathered together, it was to dispute and discuss my mother in a negative way. I always encouraged them to believe that she was a good person despite her drug addiction. Because of the positive view I held of my mother, my family began to hate me, namely my grandmother, uncle, aunt and in-laws. It was amazing to see how much gratification they got out of discussing my mother. I often thought to myself, *Wow, these people must really hate my mother and me.*

The only positive and supportive family I had was Uncle Andrew, and my older cousins: Daniel, Tricia, Carl, Elizabeth and their spouses. After months of constant arguing, quarreling and fighting with my grandmother, uncle, aunt and their spouses, my mother was finally released from jail. I eagerly awaited and anticipated being reunited with her and becoming one complete family. Once my mother was released from jail, she moved in with us at Grandmother's house. Contrary to my long-awaited hope and belief of being restored to my mother, I remained in my grandmother's custody. And I was heartbroken when she started smoking crack cocaine again. Although this was discouraging, I continued to love my mother with an enduring love that was unconditional.

At times, my grandmother would pressure her to regain full custody of us. But my mother was unable to support us financially or move my siblings and me into a house of our own. Nevertheless, when my grandmother received her payment of food stamps and the welfare check every first of the month, she often recanted her objections of us remaining in her custody. So, this roller coaster rhetoric from my grandmother continued for the remainder of my young life. She also continued to be verbally, mentally and physically abusive to my siblings and me.

My mother spoke strongly against her behavior and told her that she needed to treat us properly. Because of this opposition between them, she kicked my mother out. As she had nowhere else to stay, my mother began to live from place to place, spending the night wherever she could find shelter. The reality that my mother was now homeless burdened me deeply.

It sickened me when I saw that this fact overjoyed the hearts of my uncle, aunt, and their spouses, as well as grandmother. They would gather together, practically celebrating and discussing with the highest level of satisfaction the hardships of my mother's life. They would say one to another, "That Jackie is one sorry motherfucker," "Jackie ain't shit," and, "She ain't nothing but a damn crack head whore and her sorry ass kids ain't gonna be shit just like their sorry ass momma..." They would laugh when they followed up with, "What a shame." To add insult to injury, they would pause from this bashing and invite my older brother, Charles, and me into their conversation. They would tell us how sorry our mother was, meaning she was worthless. They certainly didn't mean sorry, as in 'feeling or expressing sympathy or empathy', as defined by Webster. I would consistently protest her with a contrary such as, "No she ain't! She means the world to me and I love her." I was not shy about openly pledging my allegiance to my mother. I made it clear to my family that they would never affect or change my view of her. This made them hate my mother and me even more passionately. Even to this day, this is true.

At times, Charles would give in to the pressure and agree with them. I hated when he gave in to their hatred because it made them extremely happy when he agreed with them. He used to joke and tease me about my faith and hope that our mother would, one day, get her life together and rescue us. Even today, he occasionally refers to the unconceivable love and unwavering faith I held for my mother.

As I think back on those times, I find some humor in the playful jabs my brother threw at me. In retrospect, I can say I was quite ignorant of the power of addiction. But I cannot say that if I were knowledgeable about the power of addiction, it would have changed my view of my mother. I refused to stop loving or expressing my love for her. Although Charles loved our mother as much as I did, he did not voice it as much.

Night fell quickly as my mother gathered her belongings and walked away to find shelter. It was a horrible feeling, watching that woman leave. My heart was pierced with the gripping fear that the abuse Madea inflicted upon me would only increase. Now that my mother was gone, I had no one to protect me.

I went to bed and awoke early the next morning for school. I boarded the school bus and the driver followed his bus route into the town of Glendale. Soon, the bus was driving into Glendale's high crime and drug-infested area everyone called the "Trap" to pick up a few kids on his route. When we drove through the Trap, all of the kids were looking out the school bus window at the multitude of people littering the street at seven in the morning. Among those people was my mother. I was saddened to see her out there in such a violent environment. I wanted to shout or wave to get her attention, but I was too afraid of being bullied by my peers. I sat in silence as we drove away.

Every morning, as the bus passed through the Trap, I would fix my eyes on the place where I had seen her standing the day before. Every morning, my eyes would drink in the sight of her. Every morning, as the bus drove away, I would watch her steadily until I could no longer see her. Jackie Jean Williams is the single most important person in the world to me. This woman and I have endured and experienced so much together. I love you, Mom.

Meanwhile, at my grandmother Madea's home, her verbal abuse quickly turned into physical abuse. I remember well the first time the abuse started. I was running from Madea, so she could not beat me. She hollered at Uncle Andrew to catch me. He tackled me and held me down until Madea could make it to our location. In her hand was an extension card. She beat me multiple times across my back and arms with it. I had no idea why she was beating me. Neither did Uncle Andrew. I can only assume that she did this simply because she felt like doing it. No one stopped her.

Some mornings, I would be sound asleep and suddenly be awakened by water pouring over me. If it were during the winter months, Madea would usually pour freezing water on me. If it were in the summer months, she would douse me with hot water. There were times when she would have my uncle hold me down so that I could not escape while she beat me for no apparent reason. When I would shout and scream for her to stop, it only seemed to provoke her into beating me more intensely. I learned to be strong and held back the tears. I wept within my soul. It was as if my inner spirit cried for me, so I did not have to cry anymore. I tried on many occasions to gain Madea's love and affection but was unsuccessful. I often wondered if anyone other than momma was capable of loving me.

After she got kicked out of my grandmother's house, my mother would frequently visit us there. Every time she spoke to us, she would tell my siblings and me that she loved us. My mother's reassurance and affirmation of her love for us enraged my grandmother tremendously. My grandmother, uncle, aunt and their spouses believed that our mother did not love nor care about us. Often, my older brother would agree with their sentiments.

The truth is our life was torment and I could not imagine anything worse. As I have gotten older, I have come to understand that regardless of how bad one's life may be, there is always someone, somewhere, that has it a little harder. To all of us that have endured such struggles, I celebrate your perseverance, and your ability and will to survive. Our overcoming spirits will perpetuate us into our long-awaited destinies.

I recall vividly the time I met some relatives from my grandfather's side of the family. I had just laid down after a long day at school. My Uncle Andrew walked into my room and asked, "Hey there, Brad, do you want to walk up on the Hill with me?" Madea had a fig tree behind her home and she would occasionally have Andrew pick some for Aunt Rebecca. He was going to take Aunt Rebecca some figs and was inviting me to walk with him. She lived only a few miles away.

I eagerly replied, "Yes!" and hopped off the bed. I was happy to hear that I had other relatives nearby. As we walked, Uncle Andrew told me that my grandfather, Isaiah Williams, had many relatives that lived on the same lot of land as his sister, Rebecca. Many people referred to that area, or small community, as the "Hill". We walked down the street from where we lived and when we reached the roadway, we turned left and proceeded to walk uphill the rest of the way. I believe this is how the Hill got its nickname: it sat on top of a huge mound.

As we walked, I wondered what they would be like. I recalled my mother telling me about my family on the Hill before Madea got custody of my siblings and me. Although my mother had spoken with high regards about my family on the Hill, I was still a bit apprehensive about meeting them. I wondered if they would be cruel and mean like my immediate family, or if they would receive me with openness. We soon arrived on the Hill where many of my grandfather's relatives resided.

The Hill consisted of about five homes on a three-acre lot, with three homes on the left and two on the right. To the left of the driveway was an old store. To the right was a large, open field with a dirt basketball court in the middle. Aunt Rebecca lived in the first house on the right. When we arrived, we saw her standing in her doorway. Uncle Andrew handed her the bag of figs. Aunt Rebecca was looking closely at me as she reached for the bag and thanked my uncle. Then, he finally introduced the two of us. "Brad, now this is your Aunt Rebecca. Aunt Rebecca, this is Brad, Jackie's son." Aunt Rebecca smiled and remarked that I was a handsome boy, saying that I looked like a Williams. That was one of the first times someone had said that I was attractive. I was so used to hearing my grandmother tell me that I looked like an ape and rant about how dark-skinned I was. Aunt Rebecca told Andrew to take me to meet Cassandra before we left. Aunt Rebecca went back into her home carrying the figs Andrew had given her and we proceeded to Cassandra's house.

Upon meeting Cassandra, I was overwhelmed by the warmth with which she received me. She hugged and kissed me while telling me how she helped to raise my mother. She told us to come inside and have a seat. Her daughter, Gail, and her son, Harry, were there, as well. Gail and I hugged one another and I shook Harry's hand. They were grinning at me and I smiled back; can someone say cheese? I felt like Whoopi Goldberg's character, Celie, from the movie The Color Purple after all the smiling. I was speechless because I did not think someone could be so deeply moved or happy to see me, other than my mother. They asked some pretty general questions, such as my age and grades in school. All too soon, Uncle Andrew told them we had to leave because it was getting late in the evening. I left with a keen sense of belonging after meeting my relatives on the Hill. We walked back home.

Upon our arrival back home, Madea appeared angry and asked Uncle Andrew what took us so long to get back. Uncle Andrew told her that I had met a few of my relatives and visited with them for a while.

Madea said, "Y'all know them motherfuckers on that Hill up there ain't a bit of good and y'all need to stay y'all sorry asses from up there." It seemed I had discovered some people—other than my mother and me—that Madea hated.

The violence and hostility Madea held for me intensified. One morning, I was lying in bed when Madea burst into the room and threw a cup of hot water on me. After she did this, she continued to walk past me as if she had done nothing wrong. I got out of the bed, drenched, and then closed the bedroom door to remove my wet clothing. This kind of behavior speaks to the very core of who I am today. Madea's abuse awoke an inner desire to be a great advocate for love, peace, and generosity. I just wanted to be loved and to love as any child would. Sadly, this affection eluded me continuously, and I never enjoyed that type of bond with anyone aside from my mother.

When I lived with Madea, I was not allowed to wash my clothing. Occasionally, I would get the opportunity to sneak a few items in with my Uncle Andrew's laundry. I was not allowed to open the refrigerator, either. My Uncle Andrew or sisters would have to open the refrigerator door for me if I was hungry. Then, I would have to stand inconspicuously at a distance in order to look inside. They would say things like, "There isn't any more leftovers in here. Madea must have hid the food from you again. Do you want this can of sweet corn?"

I would sigh and answer with my usual, "Yeah, I guess so. That's better than nothing at all." And I was right. Eating stale, week-old grits and sweet corn was better than nothing. There were many days that passed when I did not eat anything.

by Brandon Williams

I recollect bringing home over a half-dozen eggs that someone had given me. I was so hungry that day. I placed them in the sink, washed them off and grabbed the largest frying pan Madea had so I could cook them. I was not going to try to save any of the eggs because I figured Madea would throw them away. The burner on the stove was glowing and the butter I had used to grease the pan was crackling. All I had to do now was crack my eggs into the pan and scramble them a little. Before I could start, Madea came storming into the kitchen from nowhere, yelling, "What the hell you doing fool? Get out of my fucking kitchen, you black ugly bastard! Get out of here…you 'ol' black gorilla!" I stood for a second, motionless, thinking, *well, what the hell about my eggs?*

I walked away slowly, just nodding my head. After a moment, I turned around and went back into the kitchen and confronted Madea. I asked her two things: What was her problem with me? And what did I do to make her hate me so much? I told her that I did not go into her refrigerator, and that someone had given me the eggs she would not allow me to cook. She looked at me and laughed while calling for my Uncle Andrew.

"Andrew! Andrew, come here and get Brad! He out in the streets begging people for food! Tell that son of a bitch to stay out of my kitchen!"

My Uncle Andrew came into the kitchen and waited until Madea had walked away. Then he opened the refrigerator, reached behind a head of lettuce and took out a package of lunchmeat Madea had hidden. He took two or three slices, placed them between a couple slices of bread and handed it to me. I took the sandwich and walked out the back door so Madea would not get upset with Uncle Andrew for giving me something to eat.

My Uncle Andrew was a very nice and quiet man. He was mentally challenged and never received an education of any kind. Uncle Andrew never had a female companion, and I believe this was partly because of his mental handicap. Instead of spending his time chasing and wooing women like an average male in his late thirties, he devoted his life to essentially being a home health aide for Madea and my grandfather. He lived in Madea's house with us, helping her and taking care of my grandfather, who was paralyzed. Uncle Andrew had an agreement with Madea that she could keep his government disability check, but that she would give him cash when he wanted to go out and have a good time at the bar. Although Uncle Andrew never dated, he enjoyed drinking his share of beer and frequenting the local nightclubs. This mostly amounted to him pulling into the parking lot and nursing a can of beer for several hours. Then, he would return home after having made little to no contact with the other club goers.

Despite his loyalty and unusual commitment, Madea would become argumentative with him if she believed he had done something kind for me. There was a time when Uncle Andrew asked Madea for money and she told him no because he had not listened to her and was too nice to me. Whenever Madea caught Andrew giving me something to eat, she would punish him by not allowing him to receive the portion of his check they had agreed upon. She would also take the car keys so he could not go out on Friday nights. She treated him badly, and I felt responsible when my uncle was not allowed to go to a bar or get his designated portion of his check.

My mother came to visit us one day and asked if I had eaten anything. I told her that I had not. When she asked why, I told her the truth: Madea did not allow me to eat unless she felt sorry after starving me for a certain period of time. My mother and Madea got into a bad argument, shouting back and forth. It ended with Madea screeching, "Fuck you, bitch, and suck my pussy and to hell with you, whore... Damn crack head." The door slammed shut. My mother bolted and I ran out behind her. As we left, we could hear Madea shouting, "And don't you bring Brad ugly ass back here either... You 'ol' tired ass bitch."

Mother and I walked down the street until we reached the main highway. She made this cool hand gesture with her arm stretched outward, her hand curled into a fist and her thumb pointed vertically in the air. Soon, a car stopped and we got a ride into Glendale. At the time, I thought that I had learned a clever trick and knew I would use it to summons a ride whenever I desired, not fully aware that we were 'bumming' or 'catching a ride'.

We arrived in the town of Glendale and went to the Trap, where we spent the remainder of the day. This was one of my very first times hanging out in the Trap for a prolonged period of time. As the evening progressed and night fell, the more volatile the area became. People poured into the street. Competing drug dealers sized one another up as prostitutes jockeyed for their next customer. Life in the Trap was similar to any other ghetto or drug-infested area in America. Everybody was hustling in some shape or form. Everyone was in search of something in that destitute land, each hoping for riches and wealth. The evening drew to its end and now my day was spent. It was late at night when my mother decided to call Madea. We walked to a pay phone where she called and begged her to allow me to return. Madea refused, leaving my mother and me without shelter.

We walked to old man Cooper's house to spend the night. Many of the female drug addicts and prostitutes also found shelter in his home. The old man was a very good fellow, but he certainly was not a saint, nor did he claim to be one. I suppose his perverted motives were partly the reason why he allowed the women to stay at his residence. In exchange for giving them a roof over their heads, he would often call one of the ladies into his bedroom and ask for sex or for her to arouse him in whatever way an eighty-plus year old man could be sexually stimulated.

I woke up the next morning and watched the school bus pass. I should have been on that bus. I sighed and lamented, "Good grief, I can't even go to school." As time went on, there were many days like this where I could not attend school because I had spent the night in a strange place or had been on the street all night. I was on the corner in pursuit of love, security and honor. A wise man once said, "There is no honor amongst thieves," but what about killers, drug dealers and prostitutes? Was it possible for me to find love there? What about honor? Could it be found there as well?

The first few weeks I missed school, I thought it was kind of fun that I did not have to go. My mother knew my circumstances and, therefore, did not force me to go to school. She did not question me when she knew I had not bathed or been to school in weeks. However, as time progressed, missing school became a disappointment for me. I used to get lectured daily by several prostitutes, one in particular (you know who you are), about life. Many of the lectures I received were about making a better effort to attend school in the face of my circumstances. I started yearning to be in school and to get an education.

Some of the prostitutes were my mom's friends. Soon, they were my friends, as well. They were good to me. These ladies were like godmothers or guardian angels as they watched over and protected me whenever Momma was not around. They were the love, security and honor that I found on the street. It is amazing where one can find the treasure of love. Sometimes, the most compelling and magnificent possession can be found in an uncommon place. After a couple of months, Madea allowed me to move back in with her.

It only lasted for a few weeks.

Livingroom/Bedroom

Bathtub/Toilet

Bathtub/Toilet

Bathtub/Toilet

Bathtub/Toilet

Toilet

<u>Bathroom Sink</u>

Bathroom Shelf

Bathroom Shelf

<u>Bathroom Ceiling</u>

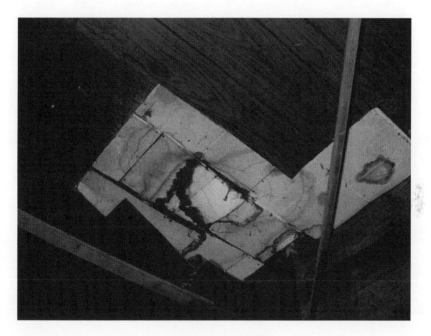

Bathroom Ceiling

Bedroom Ceiling

Bedroom Wall

Kerosene Lamp

Kerosene Lamp

Metal Foot Tub, Used as Bathtub

Metal Foot Tub, Used as Bathtub

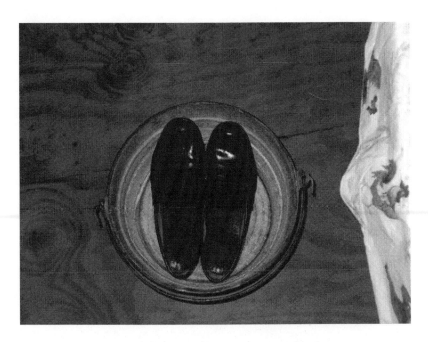

Metal Foot Tub, Used as Bathtub

<u>Doorway</u>

Self-Service Diesel Pump, Used in Kerosene Lamps

Jail

Wooded Area

Angels of the Night

My grandmother eventually forced me to move out again. I moved into an old, rundown, abandoned structure located directly across the street from my grandmother's home. Most people would just call it a shack. Once upon a time, this old house was in much better condition. Many years before, Madea had raised my mother and her siblings there. When I was much younger, I spent a few nights there before Madea moved into the trailer directly across the street. At that time, the house had running water, lights, gas and other essentials for a home to function. Now some family friends—an elderly couple living in New Orleans—owned the shack. Madea was not responsible for paying rent.

My new home did not have running water, electricity, or gas. I could not walk into the kitchen and prepare food to eat. I was unable to use the toilet when I needed to, or draw water for a bath. As I was living without water, lights, or gas, I naturally assumed these necessities would be met with the assistance of my grandmother. Needless to say, life became even more complicated while living in that shabby structure I called home.

Later in the day, I walked inside the old shack to rest. I lay down across my bed and stared at the ceiling. The old, shabby structure was literally falling apart. It was utterly dilapidated. The floor was treacherous with holes. The walls were filled with holes, as well. Many of the windows were broken or had fallen out. It had three bedrooms that Madea used for storage, so they were filled with various junk. The washroom, kitchen and living room were also decorated with clutter. There was one bathroom: A breeding ground for mold, bacteria and other dangerous microorganisms. The bathroom floor was wet, smelly and visibly unlevel. The toilet was partially sunken into the rotted floor. The base and inside of it was stained a greenish black color. The bathtub was rusty and its base was mold infested. There was a black water hose where the faucet belonged. The windows had been replaced with a clear plastic covering. There were huge holes in the ceiling. As for the smell... I would have to ask you, what smell? I was nose-blind to the disgusting odor.

The outer extremities of the shack were even worse. The tin roof was retracting and disassembled. Underneath, a great portion of the roof's wood was decayed and had been eaten away by termites. The white shingle siding was now green and scattered thickly on the ground, as the faintest breeze would cause them to fall from the house. You could see what was left of the insulation through the holes in the walls. And the foundation was nothing more than broken concrete cinder blocks. A small forest of weeds, briars and piles of rubbish surrounded the structure. My body was crushed by the brutality of the winter months and scorched during the blistering summers. I was in poor health during the time I lived there, mainly during the winter months.

After a couple of minutes, I got to my feet, went to the door and looked out across the street. I saw my Uncle Andrew walking behind Madea's house and called to him, asking him to come over for a moment.

"What did you cook for dinner?"

He replied, "We didn't cook nothing this evening, Brad."

When I asked if there was anything to eat at all, he told me he could warm up some leftover grits they had planned to throw to the dogs. I laughed and told him "Yeah… Yeah, man, give me that. Hell, it's better than nothing." He walked back across the street. Soon, I could hear Madea fussing, "What the hell that black gorilla wants? He always starving. He need to go where his momma at and ask for something to eat." I thought the madness would never cease. Uncle Andrew did not bring me the dog slop (grits) right away because Madea would not allow him to give them to me. I finally went back to my bed and lay down. Hours later, I heard a loud growl. Before I could get up to see where the sound was coming from, my stomach growled again. Frustrated, I got out of bed, walked across the street and knocked on Uncle Andrew's bedroom door. When he opened it, I asked what happen to the grits he was supposed to bring me. Madea had thrown them away when she found out that he was planning to give them to me.

"Okay." I walked back to my shack and prayed to God for a better life. I went to sleep with a hungry stomach.

The next morning, I awoke to the smell of breakfast. I love to eat bacon, although I hardly ever ate any, or anything else, while living across the street from my grandmother. I smelled bacon cooking, but instead of being mentally broken down, wondering if I was going to get to eat breakfast, I stayed inside and pretended not to be hungry. I did not walk across the street and beg for anything to eat that morning because I saw my Uncle James and his wife Lauren sitting on the porch with Madea. I knew the moment I went over to ask for something to eat, it would give them something to talk about.

One would think, with the government giving Madea over four hundred dollars every month in food stamps to purchase food for us, I would not be starving. In addition, the government awarded her several hundred dollars in a monthly welfare check to help support us. Yet, I was starving.

My desperation meant that I often went through spurts of hustling. During the days that I hung out on the block, I started selling crack, among many other illegal narcotics. Each time, I would make just enough money to buy food, clothing and school supplies for my siblings and myself. Once I had accomplished those goals, I would always tell myself that I was getting out of the dope game. Life became more complicated when I found myself at a crossroad as I contemplated whether or not I should be selling drugs. At that time, I really did not understand the game and made little to no money. My desire to stop hustling battled with the need to eat; if I stopped, I would have to depend primarily on Madea to eat. So, within a few days or so, I would normally start back selling crack. My unassuming, early stages as a drug dealer were ironic. I approached a known drug dealer named Kevin at the corner store. Kevin frequently sold crack to addicts including my mother. He wholesaled crack and cocaine to a number of lower-level drug dealers. "Yo what's good big homey... I'm trying to get a twenty-dollar flipper." Kevin asked, "Are you smoking crack?" "Man, I'm trying to sell. I'm not smoking nothing!" He took my twenty dollars and gave me forty-dollars' worth of crack cocaine in return. I walked away with two tan crack rocks valued at twenty-dollars each. I sent a random crack addict into the store to buy me a forty ounce of Olde English 800 beer. I leaned against the wall and opened it. After a few minutes passed an addict came over and asked if I had some work (crack). So, I pinched off a five-dollar piece or a nickel from one of the rocks I scored earlier. I sold him a nickel rock and he smoked it right there on the spot. He was floating on cloud nine. I made about sixty-dollars from that flipper. And the rest was history, I ultimately worked my way up to wholesaling crack.

One time, someone close to my mother died and she wanted me to go to the funeral with her. I declined, saying I was too busy hustling to attend a stranger's funeral. My momma told me that if I went to the funeral, I could eat the food they served afterwards. After hearing that, I told my momma I would love to go. When we arrived, she mingled and introduced me to several people. She would say, "Yeah, this is my baby right here, girl... You remember Brandon. He was a little baby the last time you saw him." People would normally respond with a startled look and ask, "That's Brandon? The one by Jason? Oh yeah, that boy show has grown up."

We all sat down, and I waited patiently as the eulogy was preached and the deceased was laid to rest. Now it was game time. I ate the food that was given to me, as did my mother. We even took plates to go. You see, that is the kind of thing that I loved about my mom. She was not ashamed of anything. We crashed a couple of other funerals or, to speak more accurately, I crashed them. My mother would go to the funeral because she knew the people and genuinely wanted to pay her respects. On the other hand, I had an agenda.

My mother and I have a special bond and were very close at that time, perhaps even closer than we are today. We spent most of our time together in the street. We did many fun and crazy things. But I never drank alcohol or sold drugs on the same corner as my mother. I was always serious and on guard whenever we shared the same block, although there was one exception.

One day, my mother and I had been on the block all day and it was dead, that is to say, nothing was happening. I did not have any crack to sell or any money to score drugs to resale. Momma did not have any money to buy cigarettes or beer for herself. There was no one else on the block that day, which was highly unusual for a high drug and prostitution area. We ended up in the parking lot of a store where dealers sold crack and other drugs. We walked to a tree that shielded us from the beaming sunrays. Momma sat on a milk crate and I sat on top of a wooden plank I had placed across the top of a large metal barrel.

A cousin of ours drove up, parked his truck and started walking into the store. "Chris! Chris, come here! Let me holla at you for a second!" Mother shouted. He gestured to her, letting her know he would come over once he was done in the store. After buying an ice-cold beer, Chris walked over to us.

"What's up cuz? How you doing? What's up lil cuz?" he said. He popped open his beer and Momma asked him why he did not buy more than one. He joked, saying, "Y'all don't drink! Y'all some Christians...ain't y'all?" After poking fun at us, he asked us what we wanted to drink. Mother asked him to bring her a bottle of Wild Irish Rose and I asked for some Thunderbird. Chris went back into the store and came out with two-fifths of Wild Irish Rose and a pint of Taaka

Vodka. He handed me one of the fifths' and the other to my mother. He told us to drink up and added that he would buy us more when we were done. My mother held the Wild Irish Rose propped between her legs as she opened the pint of Vodka. Somehow, my mother and I ended up in a drinking contest. Because she rarely saw me drink, she assumed that I "couldn't handle my liquor".

"Chris, that boy can't drink a fifth of liquor! We gonna have to tote him out of here."

I laughed and boasted, "I can out drink both of you any day! I can handle my liquor."

Momma gave me a startled look before grinning. "Make a believer out of me, baby."

My mother, Chris and I started drinking and trading stories. After almost an hour, Momma was working on her second fifth, but I had barely put a dent in my first. They started to laugh at me, and I laughed at myself along with them. I put my bottle to my mouth and threw it back. When I brought it back down and looked at it, I realized that I had drunk more than half of it. I continued to take big gulps until I finished it and quickly cracked open my second fifth. After a few minutes, I realized that the alcohol had started to take its toll because I almost fell off the trashcan. I nonchalantly got up and used it as a prop to keep my balance. Meanwhile, my mother continued to drink unfazed. Chris kept the fifths steadily coming. Soon, Chris was twisting open the top and passing me my third fifth. At that point, I was too embarrassed to say that I had drunk enough. When Chris and my mother were not looking, I started pouring my liquor into the grass.

My mother declared proudly, "Yes, indeed, that boy can drink." I smiled shamefully as I continued to pour out my liquor. By the end of it all, we were severely intoxicated. I cannot recall what we did next. I can only suppose that we bummed a ride to Mr. Jason Green's house. Mr. Jason was an old man we stayed with off and on in Cherry Hill, Tennessee. His house was within walking distance, but I do not think we were capable of walking there that day.

Mother and I had another unusual moment at a church in Allen, Tennessee. Allen is only a few minutes outside of Cherry Hill, which is roughly thirty minutes from Glendale. Mother and I often had deep conversations about the Lord. In fact, we did every day. Christ was our foundation and, despite the life we were living, He kept us grounded. My mother and I were on the corner early one Sunday morning when we decided that we needed a break. Mother suggested that we go to church and fellowship with other believers. So, we went to church.

Because I was hustling, I had my crack, pistol, razor blade and some other miscellaneous items on my person. When we arrived at the church, I started looking for a safe place to hide these items. I could not find a spot where I felt comfortable leaving my belongings behind. As a last-minute resort, I took my gun and crack into the church with me. I feared that if someone found my gun, they would sell it or even use it on me. I definitely did not want to take a chance with a user finding my crack because it would be smoked instantly. We found a seat in a pew just in time for the sermon.

I cannot quite remember what the sermon was about, but I can vividly recall seeing the collection plate being passed around. I noticed some people adding large bills and taking out the change they wanted from the money that was already in the plate. I kept watching the plate as it neared me. My mother quickly passed the collection plate because she did not have any money to give. When the plate reached me, I sunk my hand into it as if I had dropped a large bill and then grabbed a handful of cash, pretending it was my change. Before I could pass the plate on, Mother saw me and asked me to put the money back. I dropped some of the bills back into the plate to convince her that I had returned it. After the service ended, we exited, and mother scolded me about stealing from the collection plate.

We bummed a ride back to the corner store in Cherry Hill. Once we were there, I went inside and bought us something to eat. Red beans and rice with pigtails and fried chicken (white meat only) are a southern delight. I walked back outside, sat down under the tree with mother and gave her some of the food. "You didn't make any sells yet, did you?" she asked. I admitted that I had gotten the money from church. I told her the Lord had blessed me. She smiled and nodded her head after I told her I had kept some of the collection plate money and asked her not to be so upset with my stealing. We were in more need of assistance than anyone in that church. I concluded my argument by citing the numerous cases when Pastors and Deacons had misused church funds. Deep in my heart, I knew I was wrong, but I did not care.

When I look back on the foolish position I took in order to justify my actions, I am humiliated. I was abnormally hungry the day I was digging through the trashcan for food at the corner store. It happened while I was hanging around in front of the store. I saw a guy take a couple bites out of a piece of chicken. Then he placed the chicken into a white bag and threw the bag into the trash. I hadn't eaten that day. But it was too many people around for me to get the food out of the trash right away. I waited until the crowd thinned out first. Once this finally happened I walked over to the trashcan, looking inside. I was a bit shocked because I didn't see the bag containing the chicken the guy threw away an hour prior. Then I dug through the trash searching for it. To my dismay I couldn't find it. In the end I ate some grits Uncle Andrew gave me later that night. If I would've eaten from the trash that day it might have served as a pathway to an undesirable means of attaining food to eat.

In my teen years, I committed a lot of crimes, but I never quite got around to robbing the Exxon Mobil station in Glendale. My reason for conspiring to commit armed robbery was to acquire a generous sum of money and move my mother and myself off the streets. My plan involved carjacking a stranger and using his vehicle to drive over to the Exxon Mobil station where I would rob it. After the robbery, my plan was to flee in the stolen car and ditch it. I set out to rob that store on multiple occasions, but every time I attempted to do it, I was interrupted.

The first time I set out to rob the Exxon Mobil station, I gathered my tools and put them into my black bag. I packed a black ski mask, a black hoodie, some latex gloves, pepper spray, a flashlight, a roll of duct tape and a few other items. As for my pistol, I normally carried it on me everywhere I went. Now that I had gathered all my tools, I was ready for work.

I did not have a vehicle, so I had decided to set up a roadblock and take one. Around 1:00 AM, I closed the door of my shack and walked down the street to the main highway. I found a decayed tree that had been blown down during a storm earlier that night and pulled it into the roadway. Then I walked into the woods and waited to ambush the first vehicle that stopped. I pulled my ski mask over my face and made sure my gun was locked and loaded. After a few minutes, a car drove up and stopped just on the other side of the tree. I waited for someone to exit the vehicle before I approached it. The car door opened and I started walking towards the vehicle with my gun pointed. The overhead light inside the vehicle came on and, suddenly, I could see inside. A couple of women and a small child were inside. I shouted and cursed underneath my breath.

Lowering my weapon, I turned and retreated back into the woods, deeply distressed. As badly as I wanted to take that vehicle, I could not bring myself to rob a couple of women with a child. Although I was only a twelve-year-old child at that time, I did not think of myself as one. I watched the women struggle unsuccessfully for nearly a half hour to remove the tree until they finally gave up and chose a different route. Moments later, a truck came careening down the roadway at a high rate of speed. As the brakes were slammed to avoid crashing into the tree, I could hear country music blaring out of the window. I could see a middle-aged white fellow inside, and he appeared to be heavily intoxicated. I stalked him as he attempted to run his truck over the tree. After several failed attempts, he sat motionless for a minute or two and started talking to himself. I nearly started laughing as I approached his vehicle to extract him. When he opened his door and stumbled out, I was standing in the woods, only several yards away from him. I observed his movements carefully, pulled out my gun and ran into the roadway intent on taking his truck, cash and any valuables.

"Is that Nathan? Damn! It sort of looks like him. That's his crazy ass," I said to myself. Shocked, I turned away and re-entered the woods. Nathan was my next door neighbor; his sons and I were very close friends. Poor Nathan was too intoxicated to even notice he was in harm's way. He was somewhat of a drunk and whipped his kids regularly whenever he got inebriated. In hindsight, maybe I should not have spared him since he never spared them.

He stumbled back into his truck and drove through a ditch around the tree.

Just when I had decided to give up and was about to walk out of the woods, a car with two white hippy-looking guys pulled up. I scrambled back into the woods as they bolted out of the vehicle. One of them was giving instructions to the other as they walked toward the tree. They stopped and stood near it, eerily looking into the woods in my direction. Although I had decided that my night was not over and I would rob these two guys, the guns they wore on their sides indicated otherwise. Although I was a gangster and did not have a problem with violence, I figured I would like to live to see my thirteenth birthday. So, I quietly walked deeper into the woods and sat down.

I knew that if either of the two men heard or saw me, they would have opened fire. One of them rested his hand on his pistol the entire time they were outside the vehicle. After removing the tree from the road, they drove away. Shell-shocked, I emerged from the thickets and walked home hanging my head low. Today, I would say that the two men I described as hippies were actually narcotics officers or a pair of detectives. My plan had been foiled by a couple of women, my drunken neighbor and two suspected police officers.

I changed my plans. I decided to rob the Exxon Mobil station the next time I was in Glendale, so I would not need a vehicle to get there. Then, one evening, I found myself in Glendale, frustrated after losing almost all the money I had made selling crack in a dice game. Normally, when I lost my money in a dice game, I would pretend to be upset and snatch all the money off the floor. I often shot dice for leisure, and to earn money to buy food and other necessities. But my only problem was I never learned to quit while I was ahead. It didn't matter how much money I had won. I would continue gambling as long as someone had money. I was in New Orleans shooting dice one day and lost all of my money. I stood in silence, enviously staring at the trash talking guy that won most of my money. He stuffed the money into his pocket. He continued shooting dice with two other guys. "Seven and eight are running mates" he bragged. I reached down onto the ground between them and grabbed the large pile of cash they were gambling for. I snatched the money from them and pocketed it. They all became upset and threatened me. To which I replied "Fuck y'all. This is my money, I won this shit." There were times when I shot dice with counterfeit money I wasn't able to pass off at retail stores. When I did this, it didn't matter if I won or not.

That night, I retired from my long evening of shooting dice and got back to business. I already had my black bag with me, so I started walking to the Exxon Mobil.

It was around 10:00 PM when I walked to the street behind the store. Once there, I pulled my black hoodie over my head. Next, I removed my gun from my bag and secured it in my crotch. As I continued to walk, I heard someone running up to me from behind. I turned around and waited for the person to pass by. As he approached, I realized that it was my mother's boyfriend, Gregory. He ran past me shouting, "Come on...hurry up!" I pulled my gun out of my pants, stuck it back into my bag and started running with him. We stopped several blocks away near an apartment complex. As we caught our breath, Gregory told me he was running because he had just robbed someone.

So much for *me* robbing the Exxon Mobil station that night.

A few weeks later, I attempted to rob the Exxon Mobil for a third time. That night, I swore not to allow anyone or anything to interrupt my plans. I traveled the same path as I had weeks earlier. I climbed through a very steep ditch in order to approach the station from the rear, a poorly lit area. As I passed through the ditch, I pulled my ski mask over my face. I put on my latex gloves, and then forced my leather gloves over those. In the parking lot, less than twenty yards from the store, I stooped down behind a trashcan. I observed the movements inside and determined that there was only one clerk working. With my gun in hand, I proceeded to the front entrance.

Just as I was about to enter the store, I glanced over the parking lot. Parked on the other side was a familiar sight: My Uncle Andrew's car. I turned around and quickly pulled off my ski mask, shoving it and my gun into my bag. I shed the gloves and thrust them inside, as well. Then, I slung the bag onto my shoulder and nonchalantly walked into the store.

"Hey lil' Jackie… What are you up to?" the gay clerk greeted.

"Not too much, homey. Did you see Andrew?" I called back. Stepping back outside, I walked over to Uncle Andrew's car. There he was nursing a can of beer like he usually did. He was rocking his head to the beat of the radio.

"Hey! What's up, Brad? Where you been? Take a seat." He leaned over and unlocked the door. I sat in the car with him and he offered to buy me a bag of potato chips. We walked into the store together and I nodded my head at the clerk to acknowledge him. I grabbed a bag of sixty-nine cent Lance Barbeque Potato Chips and put them on the counter along with the snacks Andrew was buying for himself. We strolled back to the car to eat our snacks. We sat in the parking lot for a while and then drove home.

I entered my domain and Andrew proceeded across the street to Madea's. I lay across the bed and pondered deeply about my most surreal experience. The very night I chose to rob the store, I had gotten lucky because no one was there. Then Andrew had shown up out of the blue. I believed it was divine intervention that caused him to appear at that store from virtually nowhere. I decided not to rob the Exxon because I felt that God would not allow me to do it. I reasoned that robbing the store would be like fighting against God. Not a fight I was capable of ever winning. Besides, by that time, I was involved in so much criminal activity that I had grown weary of it. I had already burglarized several homes in multiple cities; I gained entry into those homes by picking the lock or kicking in the front door. Not to mention the things I did on a daily basis.

My first time eating chili was at Nathan's house. I was visiting his eldest son, Kyle, when he offered me something to eat. With Madea still fascinated with starving me, I accepted and asked him what he had to eat. He said he had cooked some chili and invited me inside. I sat on the living room couch next to a slumped over, drunken Nathan. He looked pretty much the same way he had the night I almost assaulted and robbed him. I looked over at him with a huge grin on my face.

"Hi Nathan, how's it going?"

"It's going... How about a beer? You want one?"

by Brandon Williams

He reached over and handed me a twelve ounce can of Natural Light just as Kyle brought out a big bowl of chili for me. That was a memorable day. At that point, I realized that I needed to hang out with my adopted white family more often. Nathan and I drank beer after beer and ate bowl after bowl of chili until I could not drink or eat anymore. I ate as much as I wanted without being ridiculed or stared at like a wild animal.

I enjoyed any rare moment when I could eat freely without being cursed out by Madea or looked at like a spectacle. Luckily, I was able to experience that on many occasions in many different places. I was always happy to eat anything other than those damn blackberries that grew wild in my yard or the blueberries that I stole from Mr. Coates's orchard. Later on in life, I discovered that Mr. Coates knew I ate from his orchard but did not care.

Several hours had passed and all the beer and chili were consumed. I thanked Kyle and Nathan and walked next door to Madea's house. I asked Andrew for the foot tub I used as a bathtub because Madea had hidden it from me the day before. He passed me the tub with a couple quarts of lukewarm water in it and I carried it across the street. After bathing and throwing my bath water out the front door, I rested for the night. The next day I returned to Nathan's home, unannounced. I waited until he left for work. After he was gone, I walked to his front door and kicked it forcefully. The door immediately gave way and flung open. I entered his home and searched for his shotgun. Once I found the gun, I took it and fled the premises.

I had an opportunity to start a gang called Live Nation at school. My brother, older cousins and I had formed a close-knit bond and wanted a name for ourselves. We pondered over several ideas. Eventually, I came up with Live Nation and everyone agreed to it. We got Live Nation tattooed across our backs as a vow of unity. We joked and laughed about our group. But that was all we did, with the exception of hoping to become a well-known rap group.

When I got to school, some impressionable popular kids liked the idea of Live Nation. One day, I was called into the principal's office where she asked me if I was the gang leader of Live Nation. I just looked at her and laughed. She became very agitated and insisted on an answer. I told her that Live Nation was nothing more than a name to define the bond or brotherhood that my brother and older cousins shared. I told her Live Nation was not a gang and assured her that I was not a gang leader. Then, she informed me that 'Live Nation' had been tagged in several locations throughout the school. I told her that I had nothing to do with it or with whoever was responsible. She inquired about the tattoo on my back and shook her head, abruptly asking me to get out of her office. But before I could, she questioned me about the school nurse's pager. I had stolen it but then lost it. Someone had found it and turned it in to her. She wanted to know why the pager was being paged constantly throughout the day. I told her I did not have a clue as to why the pager kept going off. I suggested that it was an alarm on the pager. She ignored my suggestion and asked if I was selling drugs. I assured her that I was not selling drugs and mocked her by saying, "A straight 'A' student like me wouldn't do something like that."

She asked me to leave and never questioned me after that.

Later, I confronted a couple of students who were rumored to be Live Nation members. They were ready to pledge their allegiance to me. And the student responsible for the tagging apologized but encouraged me to convert Live Nation into a gang because people wanted to be a part of it. I told him that starting or being a part of a gang was not my style. Quite frankly, I enjoyed doing all of my dirt alone. I never had to worry about someone snitching on me.

I had two other friends who were also drug dealers and as violent and crazy as I was. When they asked me about Live Nation, it was very tempting to have a couple of guys who were living a similar lifestyle take interest in it. Yet, I never converted my group into a gang. I considered it briefly and that was the end of it.

There was an incident on the block when two of my older cousins, a crack addict and I almost got shot. We were riding around in my cousin's car when he stopped at a crack dealer, user's house. One of my cousins got out and went to the door because he needed to collect some money that was owed to them. Unfortunately, he said or did something to the guy that he did not like, because suddenly, my cousin was racing back to the car. When he hopped inside, he asked his brother if he had his gun, to which he replied, "No!" We looked over to see the dealer storming out of his house, wielding a twelve-gauge shotgun.

I never got a good look at the guy with the shotgun and I was not aware of their business with him. My cousin sped off while my other cousin pulled the crack addict over himself like a human shield. I was in the worst spot because that lunatic was approaching our vehicle from the rear. I slumped over in the back seat to avoid being shot. Luckily for us, this guy must not have had any intentions of killing us after all; he never squeezed off a single round.

For some strange reason, and to my knowledge, no one retaliated against that guy. Both of my cousins were notorious criminals. In fact, they seemed to love living a thug's life. I was more upset with them than the nut. Otherwise, I would have gone back and killed him that day. But it was not my fight. I was happy he did not shoot because I was, most likely, the one to get hit. More bizarre than anything was the addict my cousin had used as a human shield. The addict was proud to do it! I do not quite recall the addict's exact words, but it was something to the effect of, "Boy, I saved your life, man! Now you owe me a big piece of rock for that shit." I looked at him and shook my head.

by Brandon Williams

We made it safely to the corner store in Cherry Hill where I exited the car, gave my cousins fist pounds and told them I would hook up with them later.

Student life became increasingly challenging because my life away from school was in ruins. As time went on, I became more distraught and resentful. I was twelve years old and in the sixth grade at Glendale Middle school. I was a very nice kid, but I hated going to school.

During my seventh and eighth grade year, I simply dropped out of school. I hung out on the corner with my mother instead. I loved to be with her. However, I did not quit school to hang out on the corner, I quit because I was homeless. I did not have a place to stay. I rotated between spending a few nights with my cousin Tricia, my abandoned shack and in other various places. I tagged along with my mother on the poverty-stricken streets of multiple cities. Both times I dropped out, those were my living conditions. Unlike my classmates, normal kids concerned with homework assignments and doing well on spelling bees, I was troubled over what I was going to eat and where I was going to sleep that night. By the end of my seventh-grade year, I discovered that I had been promoted to the eighth grade. I was very excited and had a feeling of happiness, indescribable in words. I had a sense of pride, despite the fact that I was homeless. At the start of my eighth-grade year, I attended class on the first day. The pressures of my personal and family life never relented, though. I continued to pursue my education, but the reality of my conditions spoke louder than my fantasy of completing school. After only a few weeks into the school year I eventually dropped out for the second time. I still hoped to be promoted to the ninth grade.

Instead of learning math and science in the classroom, I learned the science of cooking crack. I never thought that I would be a drug dealer; it was not something I wanted to do.

Although many youths today view this sort of lifestyle as a fad or a cool thing to portray, I understood the consequences early on. I never really considered myself to be a bad guy, gangster, robber and definitely not a drug dealer. But the truth is, I was all of those things. When I first started hanging on the street corners and drug-infested areas with my mother, the nice, well-mannered young man she had brought me up to be accompanied her. Initially, when I saw how life was in the streets and how the people there treated each other, I was shocked.

In areas rich in crime, drugs, and violence, real love, peace, and respect was absent. You cannot stand on a corner with a prostitute advocating love while she solicits sex in exchange for currency. She is poised and focused on making money. It makes no sense to ask a gangbanger about finding peace and about stopping the violence because he might pull out his piece and use it on you. How can you teach a drug dealer to respect the black men and women he abuses when he, himself, is a victim of that same abuse? I was in awe when I realized that life had so many twists, and when I thought I had it all figured out, it surprised me again. I lived in the midst of the ranks of these men and women. I was not ignorant to their wrongs and faults, but felt sorry for them. Many drug dealers not only think they are unstoppable, but also believe they will never get caught by the local authorities. Although they are threatening and intimidating, these guys are as feeble as little infants because they are blinded by ignorance. They are blinded by the financial gain of crack sales, and that same allure will be their downfall. This fate awaits the prostitute, the pimp, and all the others.

I still contended to do no wrong. I observed, with a trembling uneasiness, the lack of respect my mother received on the streets. I was familiar with this pain as my own family practiced this same hatred towards her, as well. This made me grow wary and very contentious of anyone who opposed her. In my heart, I was my mother's little protector, like an archangel.

I knew full well that my attitude was not threatening at all and, if anything, encouraged people to mistreat and disrespect my mother. Once I realized this truth, I had a turning point. I stopped being so nice, because nice people got killed in the street. Nice people get raped, robbed, conned and buried. So I decided to develop into the kind of people that surrounded me.

Whenever I kept the company of killers, I, too, would be willing to kill. If I were in the company of thieves, I would be prepared to steal (take) their lives. When around people that might possibly hurt my mother, I would have premeditated on how I would hurt them first. I became my environment. I became the drug dealer. Yet, I always remained respectful and compassionate towards women and people who posed no threat to my mother and me.

I lost myself in the street. I believe that's what it took to protect my mother and myself. People suddenly began to realize my new attitude, and for those that were not convinced, I convinced them. I was lost and did not even know I was missing. If I had known, I would have gone searching for me.

Meanwhile, school continued and I was receiving failing grades because of my prolonged absence. One day, while on the corner, one of my mother's closest friends encouraged me to return to school. We were sitting on a couple of buckets watching the school bus go by. She told me that regardless of how I was behaving, I was still a good person. She told me the life I was living was not the life God had chosen for me. This woman was a prostitute and addicted to crack. With pride and prejudice absent, I listened and heard her plea. I respected her with the same respect I demanded for my mother. Of course, I did not have full confidence in the things she told me. As I sat there on my bucket, I thought for a moment, *Wow, this sounds good, but I'm still homeless.* Later, I spoke with my mother about the conversation and she was elated. We decided that, in order for me to get back in school, I would need a stable place to live.

Survival Instincts

That is when we decided to approach my Uncle James to see if he would allow me to live with him for a while so I could attend school. My mother and I were currently living with old man Cooper, along with several women addicted to crack. My uncle came to pay us a visit so we could discuss the matter. My mother and I were standing outside in the yard when he arrived. We stood by the passenger door of his truck and chatted. My mother asked him mundane questions until, finally, she found the nerve to ask the big question. We asked if I could live with him temporarily to finish up my eighth-grade year. My uncle answered with the most unconcerned and underwhelming response.

"I'm not sure. I'll have to get back with you regarding that."

That was the first and last time we discussed it with him. We knew my uncle and the rest of our family hated us. But since we were living in the street and had been homeless for quite a while, we thought that even a heart of stone would be softened by our plea for help.

But this setback did not stop me from going back to school. I spoke with my principal, explaining that I had a family emergency that caused me to miss the number of weeks. Thankfully, Principal Wesley allowed me to attend class for the remainder of the academic year.

I was glad I went back to school. Now I could see my older brother every day. He and I had different fathers, and he went to live with his father months before my grandmother kicked me out of her home. The fact that I suffered tremendously living on the street, going from house to house, never affected my relationship with my older brother. In fact, I was proud and glad that he did not have to suffer as I did. He had discovered a new family with his father. He had many brothers, sisters, uncles and aunts that embraced and loved him. The only strain on our relationship was that we were not able to see each other regularly.

The unvarying beatings my mother suffered were persistent and grew more brutal. However, as I was getting older, Gregory stopped attacking my mother when I was around. I do not remember how we got there, but one drizzly day, I was walking with my mother down a highway outside of Glendale. Gregory had battered her severely and she was bloody. I tried to console her as best as I knew how. Suddenly, a truck sped heedlessly past us on the highway. Mother and I moved further into the ditch to avoid being struck. We heard the truck abruptly stop and start backing up; Mother grabbed me and said in a startled voice, "It's Gregory!"

I looked at her and said, "It's okay, Mom," as I reached back and clutched my pistol in the small of my back. We continued walking and now were near the brake lights of the truck when Gregory hopped out. He was full of bravado, shouting a variety of obscenities at my mother.

"Hey, where the fuck you going, bitch? Who's that with you?"

We continued walking forward, intent on passing him, but he approached us yelling horrible things. I told my mother to stand back while she gripped me and said the same thing. Gregory stalked over to us and grabbed her.

I stalked towards him, seething. "Take your hands off my mother, bitch… You must have lost your fucking mind, nigga!"

He stopped messing with my mother for a moment and looked at me in shock. This was my first time being confrontational with him and able to back my words with action. Gregory started to back away, asking my mother to tell me not to shoot him. He hopped back in the truck and drove away. I never even pulled my pistol.

If I would have, I would have killed him.

One of the first things I learned in the street was to never pull a gun unless you were going to use it. I had become affluent in numerous unlawful dealings: Crack sales, shooting dice, stealing and occasional burglaries were my folly. I had also grown accustomed to becoming physically violent towards others who posed a threat towards my mother or me. In addition, I had started to suffer from depression and other social disorders.

At the age of twelve, I started having suicidal thoughts. I never took action until I was thirteen. I had been out in the street all night and witnessed my mother pleading with my family to lend us a helping hand. Prior to that, I had witnessed her smoke crack for the second time, an unbearable sight. The remainder of the night, I had two constant thoughts in my mind: Kill myself or smoke crack. I thought that maybe I should start smoking crack to show my mother the negative impact it has on loved ones. I guess, in my own way, I wanted her to feel the same hurt I had felt since her addiction began.

The next day, Madea allowed my mother and me to visit. Once we arrived, we ate and bathed. There were many times like this when Madea had kicked me out of the shack. Shortly thereafter, my mother left and Madea agreed to unlock the shack so that I could sleep there for the night. As the evening progressed and night drew near, I found myself enjoying one of those rare moments when Madea was behaving graciously towards me. This happened from time to time, and I never could predict this unusual but pleasant behavior. I hung around inside Madea's house a bit longer than normal since she had graced me with such privilege.

I had stolen Madea's 22-caliber pistol, a chrome snub-nosed revolver, earlier that month. I used it for protection whenever Blacks and I set up shop or when I was hustling in the street. I took the pistol with me into Madea's bathroom and locked the door. I thought about all the horrors in my life, past and present. Quickly becoming overwhelmed with grief, I burst into tears. My body shook uncontrollably for quite some time, and I pondered if I really was worthless and going to be shit as Madea, Andrea, James and their spouses had always predicted.

I thought back to the time when I first saw mother smoke crack. I also remembered when I first realized that our lives were substandard. I knew I was living at a lower means and quality of life than the average bum. Only citizens from third-world countries paralleled my life.

I was broken on the inside. I was ready to give up. I held the gun in my hand tightly and continued to try to calm myself. The script and soundtrack of my life played in my head. The script was entitled *Failure* and the soundtrack caption read a '*Lifetime of Crying and Disappointment*'. I put the gun to my head and the music stopped.

My heart pumped harder and harder as my adrenaline rushed. I placed my finger over the trigger and stared at myself in the mirror. *How worthless I am*, I thought for a moment before deciding to kill myself. I was fed up with life and no longer willing to suffer the brutality it subjected me to. I started to sweat nervously. As I cocked the hammer of the gun, I was ready to die. Though, just as I was about to pull the trigger, I thought about my mother. I had thought about everything in my life except for her, and had decided there was nothing for me. But when I thought about her and all of the torture and suffering we had gone through together, more tears rolled down my face. My eyes were red and mucus was running from my nose. I began to think of the woman I would be leaving behind. I speculated how she would hold up after receiving the news that her "baby", as she called me, had taken his own life. How would she cope after realizing that her precious baby was no longer with her?

I knew my mother very well, and when I realized my death might prompt her to kill herself, I set the gun down. I loved my mother too much. To this day, my mother remains very loving and I know she would have killed herself or somebody else if I hadn't set my gun down that day. Too bad for the World News Network of Glendale. Senior commentators Madea, Andrea, James and their spouses would have fought to be the first to cover that story. I put the gun back into my crotch, wiped the tears and snot from my face and walked out of the bathroom.

My mother's boyfriend eventually left her for another woman. He left abruptly without notice, like he had received a letter drafting him for war. In an instant, he was gone. Several weeks passed and he never returned. Those weeks grew quickly into months, and my mother eventually took interest in another man. This guy was quite the charmer and had been begging her for a date for a while. He was a short guy, but he proudly sported an athletic build. Of course, after my lengthy experience with Gregory, I did not trust Terrence. But I respected him because my mother cared for him. The romance began and he made her smile and laugh in ways I had never witnessed. One could easily see that my mother was falling for this guy. It was pleasant seeing a woman—one who had been victimized and battered most of her romantic life—discover happiness.

There we were, my mother and I accompanied by her new companion. As awkward as it may seem, we embraced one another as one joyful family. For a time, they appeared to be inseparable. You rarely saw one without the other. The three of us temporarily found shelter at Mr. Jason Green's house, where they often walked to the corner store. Sometimes we lived in a rundown abandoned house that my mother's new companion claimed as his own. His house appeared to be in worse condition than the shack at Madea's. His place did not have lights, water, gas, and so on. His floor reminded me of a glass bottom boat because you could see through parts of it. We used to lie in our beds and watch the sunrise through the unsightly, gaping holes in the walls. I must admit that I found this quite interesting and somewhat enjoyed it. It is a beautiful thing to be awakened by the warm rays of the sun shining upon your face.

My mother would make frequent boasts to her friends about Terrence's athletic build. To be totally honest, my mother was not his only admirer. I, too, was quite the fan of this guy's bulging pectorals, enormous biceps and broad shoulders. He was good to my mother, and we were comfortably growing as a family. Out of the blue, Gregory resurfaced as quickly as he had left. He came back about three months later to proclaim his love to my mother. The sight of this man made me very afraid for her safety. Six months earlier, while defending herself against one of his attacks, my mother sustained a severed artery to her left forearm. She could have bled to death. I vividly recall my mother telling me that Gregory had cut her arm with a broken beer bottle, but later she recanted, saying she had mistakenly cut her arm herself. I know what you are thinking; that is one hell of a mistake. My sentiments exactly. The irrefutable fact about the matter was that my mother had nearly died from her injury.

The day Gregory returned, we were in Terrence's brother's truck in the driveway of Mr. Jason Green's house. I suppose we were getting ready to hang out that night or stay the night at Terrence's palace. Terrence was standing by the open driver's side door. His brother was sitting in the front passenger seat and my mother was sitting directly behind him in the rear right passenger seat. I stood there in a trance in the truck bed watching Terrence talk to my mother's crazy ex-boyfriend.

Gregory began to yell and shout louder and louder at them. What shocked me the most was that Terrence, who posed as the pillar of the community, was afraid. Gregory knew this and grew more aggressive. He tried to persuade my mother to get out of the truck by picking up a solid wooden pole about five feet long. I yelled, "Stay inside the truck! Don't get out, Momma!"

Her ex started lunging the pole repeatedly into the truck, attempting to strike my mother with it. I became impatient with Terrence when I realized that he was not going to protect her. He just stood there, motionless, only occasionally raising his arms to prevent Gregory from getting a good aim at my mother. Although Gregory did his best, he was unsuccessful each time. He kept yanking the large stick backwards as far as he could and violently thrusting it forward into the rear seat of the truck. He continued this motion several times. Each time he jabbed the stick towards my mother, I cringed, hoping he would not injure her beyond recovery. Mother tried her best to circumvent the attack, though she had limited space to maneuver. All I could see through the rear window was her outline moving about as she tried to avoid being struck as he mercilessly continued his assault on her. She folded her arms over her face to protect herself from a blow to the head.

I felt so spineless. I agonized like a powerful lion looking upon his defenseless young cub while a hyena used razor-sharp canines to attack and rip away her flesh. I yelled repeatedly at the top of my voice to

Terrence, "Man, get that mother fucker! What the fuck you doing just standing there… Stop him!"

Panicking, I looked down into the truck bed and found a tire iron. In the meantime, Terrence just stood there watching, a complete coward despite his muscular physique. Gregory remained tireless in his attempts. The truck seat and doorframe were absorbing his strikes until one finally found its way to my mother's helpless and defeated body. The bottom of my heart fell out when her piercing, painful screams filled the air as her worn body absorbed the full force of this two-hundred-plus pound mad man. I responded immediately by jumping off the truck bed, the tire iron clenched in my fist. Even though this was the first time I was physically capable of defending my mother from this abusive man, I did not know if I could be successful. What I did know was that I was the only help she had coming.

In my heart, I did not care if I lived or died that night. All I was concerned about was my mothers' safety. To my surprise, my mother's estranged boyfriend responded just as cowardly as her current boyfriend had. While I was leaping off the back of the truck, he was dropping the pole and running down the street before I even landed.

Unfortunately for him, he misunderstood my actions. I was not trying to scare him away, but was ready to inflict upon him the same kind of pain and injury he had dedicated towards my mother since I was seven. I landed awkwardly, skidding in the gravel. Even though my feet were not positioned properly underneath me, I did not hesitate in taking off in a sprint. I ran as hard as I could to catch up with Gregory. My mother began to shout, "Brandon, stop! Brandon, stop! Come back!" Her heart fluttering and gasping for breath, she continued to call out as she watched me disappear from view. Although I had grown to become like my environment and behaved as any other criminal, my mother still saw me as her innocent little boy. Her pleas for me to stop were not because she was afraid I might murder her ex-boyfriend, but because she feared he might kill me.

Behind me, Terrence had finally mustered up some courage and started running after mother's ex-boyfriend as well. Suddenly, I was thrown violently onto the ground. All I could hear were the frantic cries of my mother. I was so focused on keeping my eyes fixed on Gregory that I had tripped and fallen onto the gravel driveway. I later discovered that I had lost an eight ball of crack—3.5 grams of crack—and a couple hundred dollars, all of which had been folded into my sock. Burning with adrenaline, I bounced back onto my feet and continued to give chase.

At this point, both of them were well ahead of me and I quickly realized that I could not possibly catch up with them. As I ran, I began surveying my surroundings for an alternative route. I observed the direction they were running and realized that I could cut them off. The only thing that stood in my way was a steep ditch and a heavily wooded area about a hundred yards in depth. I soon found myself barreling into the ditch and stumbling down its vertical surface while fighting to keep my balance. I ran through the wooded area, getting whipped and snapped by its assortment of brushes, branches, and vines. As I struggled my way through the thicket, I started panicking. Despite my herculean efforts, neither Gregory nor Terrence were in sight. Just as I was screaming out, 'Damn! I lost them!' I saw Gregory careening through the woods in front of me.

My spirits rose as I watched him lose his balance and fall down several yards away. Seconds later, I saw Terrence run up. As Gregory struggled to his feet, Terrence wrestled him back down to the ground. Terrence straddled Gregory's waist, keeping him penned. I slowed down and started walking towards them as Terrence started yelling and shouting at his captive. I was disgusted with Terrence, thinking, "What the hell is this fucking idiot doing?"

I ran over and took several swings at Gregory with the tire iron, mostly striking him in the head. Terrence immediately jumped off and started running away. But I was not done. I planted my feet firmly on the ground and struck Gregory with a heavy blow. This time, it was direct and effective, landing on his face. I suppose someone could say that just as Gregory had succeeded in delivering the 'ideal blow' to my mother minutes earlier, I had landed one, as well. I stood over him in complete dominance. I raised the tire iron and struck him again, delivering the 'ideal blow' once more. The dynamic of metal and bone meeting sounded much like an axe being swung mightily into a solid piece of wood. Realizing that I had no intention of stopping, Terrence had returned and was begging me to leave. He and I ran to safety, leaving behind the man who had been responsible for torturing, dehumanizing and battering my mother for years. As I ran, the overwhelming burden of the many years of witnessing and enduring his merciless attacks lifted momentarily.

I was satisfied now that he lay in the dirt, powerless, empty and defeated. As I ran, I shouted to Terrence, "That mother fucker won't hit Momma anymore!"

We had left him there, alone and bleeding, not knowing whether he was dead or alive. We ran out of the woods retracing the path where I had gained entry, but for some reason, I did not fall or stumble leaving. Terrence and I made it to the main roadway and raced back to his brother's truck. His brother and my mother were still there, waiting for us.

My mother was shaking uncontrollably. Although I assured her that everything was okay, she continued to tremble and cry. As we drove away, Terrence advised me to throw away the tire iron. Terrence's brother stopped the truck. I got out and threw my weapon into a small pond. When I got back into the truck, my mother looked at me with a silent, unfamiliar stare, and she started shaking more violently while continuing to cry. I did not understand what was happening, but I attempted to calm her. Once again, I told her, "Everything is okay. He won't hit you again, Momma." She continued as she was for a while, but then calmed down a little once we reached my Uncle Isaiah's home in Memphis, about forty miles away from Cherry Hill. We had decided to hide at his home while we discussed and planned my next course of action. I had just murdered a man. And I was only fourteen.

We wrestled back and forth for a while with different ideas. I was encouraged to flee; my uncle advised me to leave the state. I had a distant cousin in Houston, Texas and we discussed whether or not I should move there in order to get a new start. My mother was devastated by this possibility, telling my uncle that her baby could not move to Houston by himself. Mother and I discussed turning myself in to the police. Almost everyone disagreed with that suggestion. We debated for days about what course of action would be the most beneficial for me.

On the fourth day, we left the house and were driving to the store when my mother informed me that her ex-boyfriend was not dead. When I asked how she knew, she simply replied that God had showed her a sign. She asked me if I believed her and I did. God had spoken to me as well and I believed Gregory might possibly be alive. Perhaps I was desperately hoping he was alive so I would not have to face a murder charge. When my mother and I looked at one another, I realized that she appeared to be extremely worried and worn out from what had taken place over the past several days. We talked it over some more, shared it with some close acquaintances and, in the end, decided that I should turn myself in to the police. We thought that since God had revealed to us that her ex-boyfriend was alive, I would not have to face going to prison for murder. We both prayed about the decision. She fasted. In the end, my mother had faith that I would not be incarcerated for what I had done. The next day, we were on our way to Allen to turn myself in to the local authorities.

As we got closer and closer to our destination, I began to have some doubts about all of that God talk. I said to myself, "This man is dead and I am going to jail for murder." And I knew that if he was not, I would be charged with attempted murder. My uncle's suggestion that I move to Houston suddenly began to appeal to me. I stared out of the window wondering what the hell I had gotten myself into this time. I shook my head in frustration and turned to look at my mother, wishing to tell her that I had changed my mind and was not going to turn myself in to the police. But before I could get a chance to say one word, we were driving into the courthouse parking lot. The trip had been almost an hour long, but it seemed like only a couple of seconds. There we were in the courthouse parking lot, unsure of my fate.

I became very afraid and my mother had to encourage me to get out of the vehicle. I took a deep breath and exited the vehicle while embracing her. We walked into the courthouse hand in hand as she attempted to reassure me. I began to reminisce about our times together. I thought of the moments when I was first introduced to living on the street. I recalled how sweet and innocent I was back then. I thought of the reason why I had decided to sell crack. I had suspected my mother was selling her body so she could earn the money to feed me. There used to be times when she and all of her girlfriends on the corner were broke. As we took the long walk to my fate, my mind took me back to a certain day when I was first living with her at old man Cooper's house.

My mother had looked long and hard at me, asking, "Baby, are you hungry? You haven't eaten all day! What do you mean you're not hungry?" She abruptly left the house, walking at a fast pace.

"Jackie! Where you going girl?" one of her friends asked.

"I'm about to go get my baby something to eat," she replied briskly. Sometimes, if my mother's friends had money or food, they would offer it to me, but most of the time all of us were broke. After about an hour or so, I heard her footsteps on the porch and her voice calling, "Hey girl, I'm gonna come holla at you in a minute. I got to take care something real quick."

I continued lying across the living room couch, which served as my bed, waiting until Mother walked in with a huge grin on her face. "Here, baby, I got you something to eat." She handed me a brown paper bag, saying, "Baby, this is for you." I threw my covers back hastily, sat upright on the couch and opened the bag. Inside was a can of hot sardines, a couple of slices of pepper sausage (Salami with small pieces of black peppers in it), crackers, a couple of slices of cheddar cheese and my favorite drink, a fruit punch Faygo soda.

I beamed up at my mother, mirroring the wide smile she had on her face. Systematically, I opened up the pepper sausage, cheddar cheese and the crackers and commenced feasting. I opened my soda and threw back a big gulp to wash down my food. While wiping my mouth, I noticed my mother standing near the front door, staring at me. "Eat, baby. I see that you're hungry."

I wondered if she had bought any food for herself. Curious, I asked her, "Momma, where yo food at?"

"I'm fine, Brandon. Don't worry about me. Yo momma gone be okay." At that point, I stopped eating and pretended to be full so my mother could eat. I gave her the can of sardines—one of her favorite foods—and pushed some crackers across the table to her. After a long debate about whether or not I was hungry, she took a seat and ate. She was clearly as hungry as I had been, but she always made sure I ate first, and then worried about herself later.

by Brandon Williams

There were many times like this when she would leave Cooper's house broke and come back later with food, and sometimes more than what I described. She would even have cash and after she fed me, would pull a couple of twenties out of her pocket and give me one. I regularly wondered where and how my mother got the money to buy us food. What had me puzzled for the longest time was how she had money left over after she bought it all. But once I started hanging in the street, it did not take me very long to figure out how momma was earning her money. Watching my momma hopping in and out of vehicles or walking away with men made me feel sorry for her. To my knowledge, those incidents did not occur very often, but the low frequency of it did little to ease the pain. I reasoned that if my mother was in a bad situation already, I was not going to make it worse. I sold crack and other illegal drugs to provide for the both of us. Although she never condoned me selling crack, it was obvious it made things better.

She spoke strongly against my ways, especially when I was violent towards other people. But I had decided that as long as I was known as the bad guy, no one would hurt my mother. It worked. I can say with a sense of pride that when my feet were on the same block as Jackie, nobody messed with her. If someone made that mistake, they had a clear understanding that I was more than willing to kill without hesitation. At that point, being violent was my joy. I was proud of being willing to kill or be killed. My reputation made many people respect my mother. Back in the court house, the freshly painted walls and the trustees milled about. For a moment, they tamed the anger and rage boiling within me. I took on a new temperament, one that was slow to anger; one that wanted only to be a free man. I had searched for me and found myself. There we stood together: I, myself and me. This inward unity produced sanity, which was an old friend that I seldom saw. I returned to my former loving and kindhearted self.

We were directed to a room for a preliminary hearing; before we entered I kissed my mother and told her I loved her. As we walked inside, we saw about seven men seated at a table. We sat down. They got straight to the point by asking probing questions, looking for the truth. I was silent as my mother spoke, retelling the story of her abusive relationship with Gregory. All of the men sat there and listened intently. She told the story perfectly, and as she spoke, the men seemed to become more at ease and less abrasive. But now they turned their attention to me. They wanted to hear my account of what had happened between my mother's ex-boyfriend and me. I told them in a less fashionable way than my mother, but I told the whole story as it had occurred. Well, almost the way it had occurred. I definitely did not tell them that I lost an eight ball of crack!

All of the men huddled in a corner together and spoke briefly amongst themselves. They asked us to step out of the room. While we waited, I came to terms with going to jail and being incarcerated for a long time. However, I hoped I would somehow be allowed to be free rather than imprisoned.

Soon, they opened the door and invited us back inside. We all sat back down at the table. They questioned us again, but this time they seemed to want to confirm what was already stated. We reaffirmed our testimony to the men while they cast unreadable stares over us. I could not tell if they believed us or if they thought we had fabricated the story. Both of us were scared and besieged with fear.

One of the men said, "Have a good afternoon, Ms. Jackie. You and your son are done here!" We were petrified and did not believe what we were hearing, so we both remained seated. The gentleman said once more, "Ms. Jackie, you are free to go."

My mother asked the man, "Is that it?" Then another man addressed her.

"Yes…you two are free to go… You went through enough, Ms. Jackie."

I studied the man speaking and the others as they were sitting. They appeared to be smiling at us. When we exited the room, we saw Gregory's mother, sister and a few other family members sitting on a bench. They were waiting to speak to the same men. We locked eyes with them as we passed by. One of them spoke up, "Y'all killed him. He's dead and y'all gonna be sorry."

We crossed the threshold of the courthouse exit door in full stride, walked quickly to the vehicle and drove away in disbelief. "I am a free man!" I exclaimed to my mother. She smiled and said, "Yes, you are." She told me not to listen to Gregory's family and insisted he was still alive.

We later discovered Gregory had been found the morning following the attack in an unconscious and non-responsive state, lying on the ground where I had left him. He had been taken to the emergency room where he remained in a coma and on life support for an unknown number of weeks. Apart from the facial disfigurement, he eventually improved.

Life continued on in the same manner as it had before this incident occurred. Within days after meeting with those men at the courthouse, it was business as usual. Mother was back out on the block with Terrence searching for a high. Meanwhile, I was on the street dealing drugs and milling about, searching for a way to make a dollar.

We were now living with Mr. Jason Green more frequently. Mother encouraged me to be nice to him or he would put me out because he was afraid of me. The old man and everyone in the street championed me as being a killer. I told everyone who asked me about what happened to Gregory that he had survived. But they chose to recognize me as a murderer anyway. They believed, as I had for nearly a week, that I had killed him. I could not believe so many people would embrace such violent behavior, nor could I fathom that they would rejoice at a life being taken. But when I really looked closely at the situation, I realized that those who were hailing me as a hero for my actions knew our struggle and felt our pain. Some of them were there the time Gregory almost murdered my mother. They were also present the countless times he beat her unrecognizably. They saw my older brother and I cry when she was being attacked. At times, people stopped Gregory from beating my mother, but she had no help behind closed doors, where most of her beatings took place. Who was there to protect my mother? No one could protect her, not even me.

It was amazing how people reacted to me in the aftermath of my madness. I was highly esteemed by all my fellow crack dealers, robbers, murderers, and prostitutes. Many people revered me as if I were a national figure because of my violent behavior, for nearly taking someone's life. That was like poison to me. The people around me were thirsty for violence, so I felt compelled to deliver it. They wanted more violence because they were intrigued by it. That is only a snippet of the kind of ills that have been integrated into the conscience of today's society. Sex, drugs and violence can easily be found in television, movies and in our children's video games.

My mother had suffered tremendously and had endured this brutality far too long. I personally believed that if my mother had rekindled the old flames with her ex-lover, he would have burned her to death with them. She would not be alive today if she had reestablished contact with him.

Although I had little remorse for what I did, I became paranoid and concerned about my safety. The man I had nearly killed had *many* friends who were just as violent. I normally carried a handgun in my pants or held a razor underneath my tongue for protection. This practice only intensified as I grew wary of others and feared for my life.

Even though I received great merit in the street, I was faced with the same reality that had always haunted me: I was homeless. I carried that same shame whenever I entered the school campus, as I did when I was younger. My mother's addiction began to weigh even more heavily on my heart. I even questioned myself and thought about quitting. Not school this time, but I was contemplating getting out of the dope game. I wanted better for myself, but the more I thought about quitting, the more I felt I could not quit. I knew quitting would mean no money, no respect and no protection for my mother. When someone thought of hurting Momma, they knew she had one "crazy ass son" to deal with first.

There were times when I shared the block with my mother that she became somewhat of a bully. Although bullying someone is not a favorable thing to do, I found a sense of appreciation in her actions. The hunted had become the hunter. I often interfered and talked my mother out of altercations. I did this to spare myself the trouble of having to hurt someone.

My violent and evil thoughts began to escalate. My mother often told me to love and be nice to people. I took opposition against those I knew preyed on the weak. I hated people like that because when I was introduced to the street life, I was the weak one being preyed upon. Therefore, when I saw someone being walked over or intimidated, it enraged me uncontrollably. I could not bear the sight of such turmoil. I was very affectionate to such people and wanted to guard and protect them in the same way I did for my mother.

I was successful in the street. When it came to deception, I was a master in the art. I went as far as reestablishing contact with my mother's ex-boyfriend and his family. I spoke to Gregory on different occasions because I wanted him to think I was not cautious of him. I knew I could use this to my advantage if it was needed at some time in the future. Sadly, the truth remains that I loved him just as foolishly as my mother did. The reason I loved this man was because he was the only father I had ever known. Mother's ex-boyfriend was very cunning, like most abusive men. His unearthly swagger and way with words compensated tenfold for his lack of physical appeal. Moreover, he was a very hard-working man. Even when he and mother smoked crack, he managed to hold a steady job. In fact, he took care of us to some extent when we all lived together. It was always impressive to me that whatever job he held, he was always the boss's favorite.

As a born-again laborer of Christ, I understand how God characterizes love. The worker labors after what he loves. So how did my mother's ex-boyfriend define love? And did it match God's definition?

Love is patient and kind; love does not envy or boast; it is not arrogant or rude. It does not insist on its own way; it is not irritable or resentful; it does not rejoice in wrongdoing, but rejoices in the truth. Love bears all things, believes all things, hopes all things and endures all things. Love never fails. (Apostle Paul, 1 Corinthians 13:4-8)

After observing the words of Apostle Paul, I am sure we can all agree that love is good. How do you or your spouse define love?

The love that the Apostle Paul described in his letter to the church of Corinth is not the kind of love my mother's ex-boyfriend held for her. He loved her by his own definition of the word. Let us observe what love means to an abusive man:

Love is not patient or kind; love covets another person's spouse. It insists on its own way or you take the highway. It rejoices and delights in wrongdoing, but becomes violent when the truth comes out. Love hurts all things, beats all things, betrays all things and ignores your constant cries for help. I conceal my hate with my physical appearance and my bank account. I will deceive you every time, as you are not wise enough to look beyond the surface of things. You were always distracted by my handsomeness. If I did not trap you there, my bank account and hard work ethics will bridge the gap. I mask my hate with swagger and by acting the social tycoon; I knew you would fall for that. The love I have for you is actually hatred in disguise. "If all fails, all I got to do is beg or get between your legs…then I'm inside your head." (The words of an abusive man.)

We have been made aware of some of the attributes of this counterfeit-love. We can understand love and its characterization. We can also understand how both God and abusive men define it. You should contemplate what you long for in your life. Ponder on the desires of your heart. We all want to be loved in the right way. Mother's ex-boyfriend did not love her at all. His actions said the words. His actions declared that the love he had for my mother was actually hatred in disguise.

"If the shoe fits, wear it," was something my mother used to say. But what if it does not fit? What are you supposed to do then? Imagine yourself walking into your favorite department store. You are in search of the perfect pair of shoes that you plan on wearing to a conference that night. The conference is scheduled to begin promptly at 7:00 PM and you are only a few blocks away from the venue. Unfortunately, time has gotten away from you and it is already 6:43 PM. You and a few of your girlfriends are browsing through the size eight section for something for your beautiful feet. You notice a pair of tan heels that you like. Slipping them on, you strut down the aisle; they look wonderful. While walking back up the aisle, an incredible pair of red stilettos catches your eye. Unfortunately, they are in a size seven. You check with the salesman, but they do not have them in your size. Impulsively, you squeeze your size eight feet into the size seven red stilettos and model them for your girlfriends, who are thrilled with how they look. Hurrying to the counter, you purchase them, leaving behind the pair of tan heels you had intended to buy.

At the conference, you look amazing and receive one compliment after another. After a couple of hours walking around, though, your feet are really aching. You take a seat immediately. Carefully peeling off your fabulous red heels, you are a bit alarmed to see that your toes are crooked in every direction as if they were professional contortionists. You reach down and rub your worn out, painful feet, attempting to soothe them. Just as you are thinking about pulling out the flats stowed in your purse, someone walks over and compliments you on your stilettos and inquires where you bought them. You smile and reply coyly, "These old things? I pulled them out of the back of my closet."

"You have first-rate taste! I love those heels, you look good tonight, girl." Thank you! That was enough motivation for you to forget about those flats in your purse. So you slipped those heels back on and proudly walked around in them for the rest of the evening. The mere sight of you was visually arresting. Your girls even got a little jealous because of all the attention you received. But they never knew how bad those shoes were hurting your feet. With respects to men, the message I am trying to convey is quite simple: Everything that looks good to you, ain't good for you! Would you mind being the lady enduring the conference, bearing the profound pain in those red heels? She could have worn the tan ones and looked just as good. Plus, the red shoes were knock-offs (counterfeit-love) anyway.

Mother and I started spending more time in Allen with her boyfriend, Terrence. Laughter and cigarette smoke filled the air. It was my mother and her new love. They went everywhere together. He was gaining her trust, love and affection. On many occasions, Terrence told us about a huge lawsuit he had filed after he was injured just a few months before he met my mother. He had been hurt on a job somewhere in Memphis and the company was getting ready to pay out a handsome settlement. A large sum of money like that would take us off the street and move us into a house of our own. Mother and I celebrated, telling one another our struggle was near its end. Our hearts were besieged with joy. We were happy with just the thought of having a place to live. She promised to get clean while I assured her I would stop selling crack and being a criminal. We resolved to be better people.

"Any day now, my big settlement is coming," Terrence would exclaim, a bit too often.

After a period of time had passed with Terrence talking about "when my money comes…" I began to question his story. I asked my mother if she really believed Terrence was getting a settlement. I told her I did not think he even had a lawsuit filed. Out of frustration, my mother assured me that he did. She told me that Terrence loved us and encouraged me to trust him and not to be so paranoid. I sighed slightly with my chin buried in my chest and complied, "Yes, yes, mother, I guess so."

In the meantime, Terrence and my mother continued with their passionate, drug-fueled relationship. I felt like I had taken a backseat in my mother's life for the first time. I am not saying he came between us, by any means, because that would simply be untrue. I think my selfishness and insecurity provoked me into feeling apprehensive about Terrence. The poor woman had finally found love, or so she thought, and I ought to have been supportive of her. She had found a new love, one that did not punch or kick her like the love to which she was accustomed. This was a moment of peace in our lives. The mad and crazy temperament I had developed was starting to subside. I tried to uphold some of the things I had promised my mother, like going to school more often.

by Brandon Williams

Although I missed many classes and had poor attendance, I did not quit. My mother's girlfriends seemed to trust me for some reason, though I could not figure out why. They, like my mother, thought that I was something special, and this gave me hope. I had hoped that maybe I would not be a failure in life. I had hope that someday I would make something of myself. That hope compelled me to go to school as much as I could.

Lifetime Chances

For the first time in my life, I started completing homework assignments and participating in classroom exercises. I promised Principal Wesley months earlier that I would stay in school and attend class for the remainder of the academic year. I was finally on track to realize that promise. This achievement did not change what I was faced with on a daily basis. I was still homeless, still poor and continued to sell drugs. Unlike most drug dealers, I never really had an entrepreneur's spirit. The hope of getting rich by any means was not my modus operandi. I could have sold drugs and made a lot more money, but I was at war with myself the entire time I sold crack. I often pondered the hard life I was living on the street without shelter; a direct result of my mother's drug addiction. I wondered why I would look to the same antagonist that was destroying our lives as a way to help rebuild it. Evil conception cannot produce good results.

Terrence's depiction of us living the good life after he got his settlement was nothing more than a fantasy. As time progressed, my mother began to realize this, as well. They began to smoke crack and drink more frequently. Now that Terrence had gained my mother's trust and part of mine, he became comfortable. He decided to show us the Terrence he was too clever to reveal at first.

During this time, I got together with a good friend of mine and expanded my drug operation to Memphis. The city's population is much larger than Glendale, Cherry Hill, Dover, and Allen, which were some of the areas where I sold crack. Blacks and I were very close friends and I learned a lot of things from him. I learned about the dope game and what it meant to be gangster or a "real nigga". Blacks knew all about my living situation, including my mother's addiction and that she was a victim of domestic violence. He was cool, charismatic and I enjoyed hanging with him.

One day, we went to a guy's house in Memphis to buy four ounces of cocaine. When we arrived, Blacks asked me if I had a gun. When I told him that I did not, he instructed me to stay in the car. I watched as Blacks pulled out a chrome pistol (.357 Magnum) from underneath his seat and placed it in the small of his back. I asked him, "Why in the hell are you taking that shit? It ain't even loaded." Blacks replied that he knew it was not loaded, but asked me sarcastically if the dude inside the house knew that. At that, I smiled and sat there feeling like a young rookie in street life compared to Blacks.

We were parked in front of the home of Raymond White, a.k.a. One Eye. His yard looked like a pit-bull kennel. He had dogs everywhere. Blacks exited the vehicle and went inside and came back a few minutes later with the cocaine. I eyeballed it cautiously to make sure it was roughly four ounces. I did not have a scale, so that was the best I could do. Plus, Blacks reassured me that One Eye had weighed it inside. We left One Eye's house and went back to the "trap", a house dedicated exclusively for cooking and distributing crack, to divide the product in half. Blacks took two ounces and gave me two. We tested our product on a couple of crack addicts by giving each of them a hit— about three dollars' worth of crack. After they finished smoking it, they confirmed that we had a good product. The night was young and it was time to "set-up shop"—get the word out that we had the most potent product in the area. We hung out on the block, drank a couple of Heineken's and sold as much crack as we could. Several hours passed and we decided to retire for the night.

A couple of days later, I went to my grandmother's house to visit her and my Uncle Andrew. When I walked inside, they were watching the evening news as they usually did, so I joined them. The news reporter said there had been a double homicide the day before in Glendale. There had also been several home invasions, resulting in the severe injury of one homeowner. We were shocked that such a horrific and tragic event had taken place on the good side of Glendale, as it is a small community and nothing of this magnitude had ever happened.

The reporter went on to state that the five perpetrators' original plan was to drive from Memphis to Glendale to rob a reputed drug dealer, commonly known as Big Boy. When the five arrived at the Glendale residence where they believed Big Boy lived, they discovered that he was not there. The situation escalated when one of the five men shot and wounded a man inside the home and then inadvertently shot one of his own. The suspects reportedly fled the scene in their van, but before they could leave Glendale, they crashed into another vehicle. All five men climbed out of the windows of their van and fled into a nearby wooded area, getting separated in the process.

In their desperation to get back to Memphis, three of the men invaded a nearby home in an attempt to obtain a vehicle. They approached the homeowner and demanded he drive them to Memphis. When he refused, they attempted to steal his truck. When they had trouble starting it, one of the suspects began severely beating the man with a claw hammer, ripping off one of his ears in the process. In the meantime, the two other suspects managed to start the victim's truck and escaped in it, leaving behind their fellow criminal.

Left behind by his cohorts, the lone suspect then proceeded to the next house, where the mother of the man he had just beaten resided. At the second home, the elderly woman was thrown to the ground, breaking her wrist. When the suspect was unable to find the keys to her truck, he moved on to the next house. There, he encountered an elderly couple that had been married for forty-five years. By kidnapping the two and stealing their car, the suspect was finally able to leave Glendale.

Later, the Memphis Fire Department and Police were alerted to the couple's car, which was on fire. After extinguishing the flames, the couple's badly burned bodies were found in the backseat. Both had been shot multiple times at close range.

In conclusion, all but one of the five suspects had been arrested and taken into custody. The suspect at large was the one responsible for the violence. Suddenly, a picture of the suspect, identified as Raymond "One Eye" White, was displayed on the television screen. I was stunned. This was the same guy Blacks and I had gotten our work (crack) from a few days earlier. I wanted so badly to tell them that I knew this lunatic and that I had been at his house a couple days prior to the incidents. Of course, I did not tell them anything, but sat there and acted as if I did not recognize him.

Now I fully understood why Blacks wanted some sort of protection whenever we did business with One Eye. Normally, when a drug dealer is dealing in small weights (less than a half a kilo of cocaine, but that is relative) there was not a real need to stay strapped—armed with a pistol or assault rifle or whatever weapon one can get his hands on. I sat in Madea's living room with her and Uncle Andrew, and started thinking about how this terrible event had happened. I was appalled at how inhumane we humans can become in our selfish acts of rage and violence.

by Brandon Williams

The couple that One Eye had reportedly killed was one of many across the nation who had become victims of a senseless act of violence. This grieved me. I hated violence just as much as I hated selling drugs, but I felt that I had no other reasonable alternative. Later, I called Blacks and asked if he had heard about what happened. He told me he was aware. This sort of drug-related violence occurs every day, and it can happen anywhere and at any time.

The next day, I met up with Blacks in the trap house to cook some crack. Later that day, I received an alarming phone call from a relative telling me that Terrence had just beaten my mother severely. I was told that she was walking around town with a pair of sunshades on her face and would not let anyone see her face. I knew that she normally wore shades whenever she had been beaten, so my heart began to race. My mind was clouded and I could not think clearly; I was in shock. I could not imagine this guy putting his hands on my mother after he had witnessed my attempted murder of the last man that had assaulted her. Now I was infuriated. I asked how badly Terrence had beaten her. I was told that my mother could not see because her eyes were swollen shut. I cried out loud and Blacks watched silently as I wept nonstop. I hung up and called my grandmother to ask if she knew of my mother's whereabouts. Unsure, she thought my mother might be in Allen.

Blacks and I discussed what had happened and I asked him to drive me to Allen so I could kill Terrence. Caught off guard, Blacks asked

118

me if I was serious. He proceeded to caution me about the repercussions and consequences that would follow my actions. He reminded me of what had happened some time ago when I had faced the possibility of being convicted for murdering Gregory. Blacks remarked, "So you want to kill him... Just like that? You will be looking at some serious time... Don't you already have a pending case?" I understood fully. At this point, I hadn't seen my fifteenth birthday and this was my second time deciding to murder someone.

Blacks and I discussed letting everything die down before I killed Terrence, so I would not be a primary suspect or, more desirably, a suspect at all. Although he made perfect sense, I strongly disagreed with him. I did not want to wait years or even months before killing Terrence. I could not wait that long. I had to deal with him right away.

I already had my gun with me. Unlike any other time when I did dirt (criminal activity such as serious felony crimes and misdemeanors), I was not concerned about having a ski mask and the likes to conceal my identity. I did not care if people knew that I had murdered Terrence.

Blacks parked his primary car since it was registered to him, and we switched to a stolen 1978 Oldsmobile Cutlass Supreme. This was the same car I had bought from him a few months earlier. It was also my first vehicle. My grandmother had gotten suspicious of it, so I had resold it back to him. Only God knows to whom it was registered legally. The Oldsmobile Cutlass Supreme was ideal, given that we needed a car the police could not trace back to either of us.

We stopped in Cherry Hill on our way to Allen to see if Terrence was there. The first place I went was the corner store where all the drug addicts and dealers conducted business in the parking lot. I got out of the car wearing a radiant smile. I fist-pounded and shook hands with several acquaintances. As I was performing, I was scanning the crowd for Terrence. A few people asked how my mother was doing. Some asked what I planned to do to Terrence for hurting her. I told them that I forgave him and assured them that I was a changed man. I went into the store and asked Terrence's grandmother if she had seen him. She said, "No." I got back into the car and told Blacks that Terrence was not there. We drove away and continued to look for him.

I went to Terrence's grandfather's house and knocked on the door. His grandfather came to the door and opened it a tiny bit. I reached my arm in through the small crack and shook his hand. I looked passed him into his living room and asked him if Terrence was there. He told me that Terrence had moved back to Memphis.

From there, we drove to Terrence's brother's house. When we spoke, he told me that he did not know where Terrence was. I was getting frustrated, as all of my attempts to find Terrence were fruitless. It was starting to seem as if the likelihood of me taking Terrence's life that day would be impossible.

I even went to the old rundown shack that my mother and I stayed in from time to time with Terrence. This was going to be my last stop for the day. Once I arrived, I got out of the car and approached the home. Blacks waited for me in the roadway with his car idling and the gear in drive. My pistol was in the small of my back as it had been the entire time I had been speaking with Terrence's relatives. I opened the doorway and called out for him in an unassuming, friendly way. "Yo Terrence! Hey Terrence! Are you here, man…?" I mumbled, "Shit," in anguish after realizing he may not be home. After searching the entire house, I was satisfied that he was not there. I walked back to the roadway where Blacks was waiting and told him to take me to my grandmother's house.

We pulled into her driveway and I told him I would hook up with him later. Before he left, he told me he would continue looking for Terrence for me. I thanked him and walked into my grandmother's yard, where I saw her sitting on the front porch.

She whispered, "Brad. Come here, Brad. I got something to tell you." As I walked closer, she said, "Go inside and check on your momma. It's a shame before God how bad that man beat her."

I was asking Madea how long my mother had been there when, at that moment, my mother walked slowly outside hardly moving her arms or neck. It was obvious that she could not bear the pain her body was in. She was wearing her sunshades. As always, I hated those sunshades, because I knew that once she took them off, I would see her bruised face. This time, however, her face was swollen so badly that wearing those shades did little to hide her injuries. When my mother looked at me, I burst into tears.

"Brandon, why are you crying? I fought that motherfucker back. That's right. I fought his ass back, baby." I asked her to take off her glasses so I could see her entire face. Once the shades were off, I could hardly recognize her, as it was like peeling off a new skin and exposing an old wound. She tried to make light of it by being enthusiastic about being able to see a little out of one of her eyes. Although she said it was not so bad, the fact remained that we knew it was very bad.

She walked inside the house and slowly made her way towards the bathroom. I followed her inside and watched as she stood in the doorway, looking in the mirror. I stood with her as she strained to examine the bruises on her face out of the eye she was able to reopen. We studied her blackened, swollen eyes and bloody nose. My mother had been brutally trampled. Her whole face suffered bruises and deep scratch marks and lacerations. We stood there for a while, motionless, without speaking. It was the silence of that moment that spoke to us. It told us it would heal us from the constant battery and beatings of life. My mother began to cry and I wept right along with her. I tried to be 'strong' and hold it inside, but I could not stop the tears from flowing. She would stop crying for a time and, seconds later, burst into tears again. It was a sort of therapy that released all of our anger, rage, hurt and pain.

To the women reading this story, in all honesty, have you ever worn my mother's shades? If so, the next time you are wearing them, take them off and look in the mirror. Now ask yourself a question and answer it honestly: Are those birth marks or scars all over your face? Domestic violence is one of the leading causes of injury to women, more than car accidents, muggings and rapes combined. ("Violence Against Women, A Majority Staff Report," Committee on the Judiciary, United States Senate, 102nd Congress, October 1992, p.3.)

To my understanding, this was the worst my mother had ever been beaten. We sat together and she told me the entire story. My mother and Terrence had gone to a bar in Allen. They had just arrived and were outside when he started yelling at her. Then he attacked her. Terrence's brother, Ken, ran out of the bar and stopped him. After Ken went back inside, Terrence started assaulting her again. This time, he knocked her onto the ground by striking her in the head with his fist. Once she fell down, Terrence kicked her several times. She begged him to stop, but he continued stomping and kicking her while shouting brutal insults. She said that a bystander intervened, but was unable to stop Terrence. She blacked out during the rest of his attack, but somehow managed to get off the ground at one point. She had a knife and pulled it out. Defending herself, she stabbed him in the abdomen with the seven-inch blade, concluding his vicious assault. Terrence was quickly taken to the emergency room and later flown to a hospital in Memphis.

My mother talked to me about her plans to move forward, and vowed not to stay in a relationship with an abusive man. She assured me of this and I supported her decision. I asked if she knew where Terrence was living in Memphis. She responded by requesting that I not harm or kill him. Mother knew that I would have killed Terrence had I been given the chance. That would have been as natural for me as drinking a glass of water. Just like Blacks, she referred back to the incident with Gregory. I assured her that it was over and did not plan on looking for Terrence anymore.

My mother went to the Glendale Police Department to see if the authorities in Allen had issued a warrant for her arrest. She was advised that the Allen Police had not alerted them nor had they issued a warrant. They advised my mother that if the authorities in Allen issued a warrant for her arrest, someone would be in contact with her.

Weeks had passed and there was no sign of Terrence. I waited for him like a child waiting on his father to return from a long trip. I thought that maybe, one day, he would slip up and return. I did count on him to believe that a lapse of time would mitigate his wrongdoing. But he never made that mistake. I suppose he knew, as most did, that he would have lost his life if he ever came within my reach. I contemplated looking for him in Memphis, but eventually decided not to. I was not familiar with the entire city and did not have the money or time to invest. Who knew school supplies and new school clothes were so expensive?

Nevertheless, my mother fully recovered and the soreness of her beaten body subsided. She stopped staying in the old abandoned house in Allen where we used to live with Terrence. She came back to Glendale and moved back with old man Cooper again. She and I had spent the night there many times before. Several of her friends were still living there, as well. When I was not staying there, I spent the night in Madea's old shack and kept living my dangerous lifestyle.

While living the street life, I picked up a few habits from different people. One person who influenced me greatly was my cousin, an ex-convict I will call "Slim". He used to lift weights as if his life depended upon it. This guy worked out like he was a professional athlete. I asked him once why he exerted so much time and energy into weight lifting. Slim told me he had to stay fit because of his gangster lifestyle, and he encouraged me to do the same. He explained how either one of us could end up in jail any day, or be attacked by rival drug dealers or by some random guy trying to make a name for himself. He wanted to be prepared for the worst at all times. Judging from the looks of it, he was doing a damn good job preparing. Slim looked like a sculpture. In fact, although he was a few inches taller, his physique resembled that of the late Tookie Williams, the notorious leader of the Crips street gang from South Central, Los Angeles, California. Most men in jail and guys like Slim worked out daily, conditioning their bodies to be prepared for the inevitable. Another reason why guys such as Slim trained so hard was to be more capable of effectively assaulting someone and ending the assault quickly (one hitter quitter). I started training and conditioning my body like Slim and many of my counterparts.

The school year was nearly over and I continued to attend class as much as I could. As a result of my weight training, a few of the guys and a couple of coaches on the football team tried to recruit me. I was reluctant to do so because I hardly ever went to school, so I thought it would be impossible to participate in a sport. In addition, I was a little hesitant because I did not know them and wondered why they wanted me on their team. Upon the end of the school year, I was informed that I was promoted to the ninth grade.

At last, I had finally made it to high school. I was fifteen years old and the year was 1997. Even though I was behind my peers by two grade levels, I was in high spirits to be there. After dropping in and out of school throughout the years, it seemed unthinkable that I would make it to the ninth grade.

I had gotten behind by failing to pass the fourth grade twice. When I discovered my mother was smoking crack, I stopped caring about school and everything else. I failed the fourth grade the first time because I rarely attended class. I had to at least come to school in order to have any hope of getting promoted to the next grade. The second time I was retained in the fourth grade was because I did not pass the T.C.A.P. (Tennessee Comprehensive Assessment Program) Test. Although my brother, Charles, was only one year older than me, he was ahead by three grades. Now that I was in high school and sharing the same campus with my older brother and his friends, I was motivated to stick around rather than dropout, despite being homeless. Sadly, many students set a goal to reach a specific grade level before dropping out rather than aiming to graduate from high school.

I joined JROTC (Junior Reserve Officers' Training Corp) and became well acquainted with most of the instructors. Some of them learned about my personal life outside of school, but still regarded me as they did everyone else. I appreciated them for it. JROTC was fun and I really enjoyed being a part of the program. It made me feel like I had a family. In addition, wearing the JROTC uniform every Tuesday served me well because I could not afford clothes for school. Although we were only supposed to wear it once a week, there were times when I wore my JROTC uniform twice in the same week. When my peers would ask me why, I would usually respond by saying, "I must have my days mixed up again," and pretend to be disappointed.

Occasionally, I stole some of my school clothes from places like Dillard's and JC Penney. At the time, I was not making a lot of money selling drugs because I was not really applying myself. I did not assert myself or put in the work as I normally did to make sales. I was losing my ambition as a hustler. I was broke and crack sales provided my only income. Now I was depending more on the fifty-four dollars Madea gave me begrudgingly every month from my welfare check. My interest was torn between paving a way for myself in a life of crime and getting an education. I knew receiving an education would create an opportunity to someday make an honest living, and the school year seemed to fly by quickly.

For some vague reason, my brother decided to drop out of school. I was very disappointed when he dropped out permanently, and no one was able to talk him into returning. Of course, with my history of dropping out, I was not in a position to tell him differently.

Things grew more challenging in my personal life. The street life was starting to weigh heavily on my heart. Moreover, my mom was involved in a few altercations on the block. I was attending class regularly and had stopped hanging on the corner as much, missing out on potential crack sales. Also, I still did not have a steady place to live. As a result, I contemplated dropping out for a third and final time.

I went to school and told some of my friends that I would not be coming back. News of this got back to one of my JROTC instructors. When the instructor asked me if I was quitting school again, I responded hesitantly, stuttering, "Yes, yes Sir, I'm quitting." Then he asked me why I wanted to quit school. At that point, I exposed myself completely. I shared everything I was afraid to tell anyone at school with my instructor. I told him I was homeless and that my mother was an addict. I told him I was currently living in a crack, whore house with several addict prostitutes. I shared what my life had been like since I was seven. I told him that living a life under those circumstances was very challenging and going to school only added to the burden.

He stood there for a moment in silence with a blank stare before he spoke. He said that he understood my situation and admired my perseverance. He proceeded to tell me many sincere things to convince me to stay in school: I was a good kid and he respected me. "Hopefully, things will get better for you," he said. Then he said the one thing, above all, that helped me decide not to drop out. "Your life may be hard and I do not doubt that, but quitting school would only make it harder for you in the long run."

I told him how I longed for a permanent place to live. We talked about an all boys' camp that was in the middle of Glendale. One day, my mother and I walked past the camp. When I looked inside the fence, I saw many troubled young men just like myself. I observed the boys playing basketball, lifting weights, and laughing. I told my mother I would love to go to that camp if it meant that I could be off the street. I thought I would find shelter there and perhaps some food to eat. I was jubilant about the possibility of no longer being homeless. Then I began to feel bad about leaving my mother behind. Eventually, my thoughts of leaving her diminished because the guilt weighed too heavily on my conscious.

At the time, my mother was searching for government assistance and charitable organizations that would be willing to help us. She was rejected and denied repeatedly until someone finally answered her with that long awaited *yes*. We were so happy! My mother scheduled an appointment to meet with the agency in Memphis the next day. After the meeting, she informed me that, unfortunately, we were not accepted because the agency would not accept children. I was amazed at my mother's unfailing love, despite how badly she needed shelter. In the face of all her efforts, she had told them that she could not leave me behind.

My instructor informed me that the boys' camp to which I was referring to was actually a Juvenile Correctional Center. I told him that I had eventually discovered the name of the place. In fact, knowing it was a Juvenile Correctional Center, I had even thought about intentionally committing a crime in order to get apprehended by the police and placed there. My reasoning was that at least I would have shelter and food for a little while. The school bell rang; we shook hands and parted ways with the understanding that I would return to school the next day. I thank God for Major Davison for encouraging me to continue my education. I never gave another thought to dropping out of school after our conversation.

I continued with school as agreed with a sense of liberation. I believed that, one day, my education would pay off, as my JROTC instructor suggested. Even with many mishaps, by the end of the school year, I was promoted to the tenth grade.

One day after school, I went to the Trap to check on my mother and see how she was doing. As I walked down the street, the drug dealers were dealing and the crack addicts were nourishing their cravings. When I saw my mother, she nervously told me that she might have mistakenly sold crack to an undercover cop. When an unfamiliar person wanted to buy crack and the dealers were skeptical of that person, they would get an addict to make the sell. The dealers did this in case the person was an undercover police officer. Momma often got crack from a dealer and sold it on the street. When she sold the crack, she would give the money to the dealer in exchange for crack to smoke.

In my mother's case, unfortunately, the guy with the unfamiliar face was an undercover officer. She was soon arrested for distribution of crack cocaine. During her indictment, she was summoned to Allen for a hearing and found guilty of aggravated assault for stabbing Terrence. The two charges ran concurrently and she was sentenced to umpteen years of imprisonment. With a larger portion of her sentence suspended, coupled with good behavior, she ended up spending less than four years in prison. Although I was at peace knowing that she was not out in the street smoking crack, I resented the fact that my mother was incarcerated. During this time, I faced many challenges and arrived at a turning point in my life. I was beginning to grow spiritually and had started pondering positive things to do with my life.

My family moved quickly in updating their latest lingo. While my mother was incarcerated, they stopped calling her 'crack head' and started referring to her as 'jailbird'. I believe their thinking process was wired backwards. Today, I still believe that they are depressed when my mother succeeds, but overjoyed when she fails. Madea, Andrea, James, and their spouses Lauren and Matthew, were our faithful antagonists. We could always count on them to do or say something negative about us. I have not in my lifetime witnessed a group of people more jealous, insecure or hateful as they were. Unlike my loving mother, I hated them unwaveringly. When election time nears, politicians assembles their teams and hold frequent meetings about their agenda. So did the condescending five: Gossiping about my mother was their only agenda.

The jail in which my mother was confined was within walking distance from the Trap. My first visit to see her in jail was a joyful one. We laughed, hugged, and talked as if she was not even incarcerated. I was very happy to see my momma. I looked her over carefully and told her she looked good. She had gained a little of the weight back that she had lost due to her lifestyle. Her eyes were clear and her thoughts were, too, now that she was not in a chemically induced state. We did not really discuss why she was in jail because I pretty much knew the whole story. We did discuss how her feet were swelling because of her walking on the concrete floors of the jail. I asked if she needed anything and if she had money on her books (jailhouse financial account). She said she was fine and did not need anything except some cigarettes. I told her I would put some money on her books and buy her a pack from the commissary.

My mother introduced me to a couple of her friends and I greeted them with a polite hello as I smiled. She told her friends that I was her baby, and one of them mumbled something to which my mother replied, "No, you can't have my baby Brandon." For the most part, they seemed to be fair people, despite the fact that they were confined.

I saw other inmates having their photos taken with their families and I asked my mother if she wanted to take a picture, too. She told me it cost too much money and not to worry about it. I went over and inquired about the cost of the photo and discovered that one Polaroid photo costed five dollars. This was in 1999, and many years later it only costs about three dollars to get a picture taken in other institutions.

We continued talking and our favorite topic of discussion finally came up, as it always did. Our favorite topic was "God" and it still is to this day. We shared his teachings generously amongst ourselves. We enjoyed each other's company immensely: after all, we were best friends. She was all I had and I was all she had. Besides Jesus, there was no one else; it was only mother and me. It had always been that way since I started living on the street with her. She talked about her withdrawal symptoms and how she was glad to be clean.

Our visit was about to end. We embraced one another and walked towards the exit gate. I saw a couple of inmates waiting in line to take pictures with their families. They wore gleaming smiles. I told the photo guy that I would like to have a picture taken, as well. I noticed my mother standing slightly behind me with a huge grin affixed to her face. This made me cheerful and she was, too. It is hard being poor and always being denied even the simplest things in life. My mother and I posed for the photographer, and he captured our bright smiles for the portrait. I offered the picture to my mother, but she insisted I keep it.

I left the jail walking and when I glanced back over my shoulder, I expected to see my mother walking inside. Instead, I saw her standing with her hands gently grasping the chain links of the razer barbed wire fence, staring at me as I walked away. I love that woman so much, I just cannot explain it in words. She has done so much for me. Despite her drug addiction and the abusive relationships she suffered, she is more of a mother than any kid could ever imagine. I thank God for blessing me with his very best. She is my dearest friend, my sister in Christ and my mother. I waved to her, turned forward and continued walking.

Since my mother was back in jail, it was hard for me to spend the night going from house to house as she did because I was not as willing or comfortable to ask people I did not know well for help. Instead, I started spending most of my nights in my shack across the street from Madea's house. I also found shelter several nights in the trap house in the area where Blacks and I sold drugs. That was a very dumb move on my part as a criminal. Not only could the police have raided it at any time, but armed cracked out addicts could have burst inside looking for their next fix. I was aware of the danger that surrounded me, but I did not care. I needed a place to sleep and that is all I cared about during those moments.

By the time I made it to high school, I had survived and experienced more in life than most adults. I felt mature, like an adult or what some would call an original gangster. I was growing weary of a life filled with violence and crime. I wanted to live the life of a kid. Whenever someone asked my age and I told them, they would comment that I was too mature for my age.

So I would tell them, "I'm only fifteen (or whatever age I was at the time) physically, but I'm a ninety-year-old man mentally." I was implying that I had lived a harder life and had already experienced more challenges than most do in a lifetime.

I was in the tenth grade at sixteen. I started selling crack and competing with the local drug dealers when I was thirteen. At that time, my peers were men and women in their twenties, thirties, and forties. I was not able to let my guard down with my peers out there on the street. School served as my safe place. It shielded me from all the madness I dealt with in the street. I did not have to worry about anyone pulling out a gun and blowing out my brains if I said something they did not like. I enjoyed being at peace in school. I did not have to be a gangster there.

Soon, I joined the football team, as many of my peers and coaches had encouraged me to do. I loved it. I felt a sense of belonging, like I was part of a family. I loved interacting with my fellow teammates.

In fact, I caused fewer problems in school than the typical student. I never got expelled or suspended. I only had an in-school suspension once for a few days. A close friend pushed me in a chair across the classroom while the teacher was lecturing, and then down the hallway after class ended. We were just goofing off, I suppose. I was involved in only two gang fights and nearly a third. That was all the problems I caused in school. Okay, well, I sold a little weed and carried a couple of guns to school, but that was it. I promise.

The football preseason practice progressed, and it became intensely harder and harder. The demands the coach laid upon us became very difficult for me to meet. We had to practice twice a day and, at times, in the rain. For my teammates, this was wonderful, but for me it was a nightmare. After practice, I would return to my shabby, abandoned dwelling soiled with dirt and carrying a stomachache because I was hungry.

As I mentioned before, I did not have running water in my shack and, therefore, could not bathe. Even if there had been running water, the rust-stained, moldy and bacteria-infested bathtub was partially sunk into the floor of the bathroom and would have easily fallen onto the ground if I had put one foot inside of it. The flooring in the bathroom was always damp and very unstable, like most of the shack. The odor was like living with a decomposing animal: Completely unbearable. The entire place was cluttered with piles of trash and discarded junk that Madea stored there. The walls and flooring throughout the shack were unstable. Weeds and other rubbish grew out from the cracks and holes in the walls and floors. I attempted to clear out the living room area the best I could manage. I put most of the junk into the rooms where Madea piled the majority of her stuff. I cleaned the living room when I first started living there. The living room was my kitchen, bathroom and bedroom. I lived in the living room because it was the most sanitary and in better condition than the rest of the house.

I was given a foot-tub (round, aluminum, four-gallon washtub) to bathe in. The foot-tub was very small; it was about one foot in diameter and a little over a foot tall. This was my bathtub, and since I didn't have running water in my shack, I asked Andrew for hot water to fill it with. Normally, by the time Andrew brought my foot-tub back the water in it was lukewarm and oftentimes cold. There were many times when I wasn't allowed in Madea's yard, so I couldn't get my foot-tub as soon as Andrew prepared it. I had to wait for him to bring it across the street to me. At first, he drew water from their bathtub faucet. But by the time it got to me it was never hot. Andrew and I ultimately decided on him bringing me the water after he boiled it on the stove in a tea kettle. Madea wouldn't allow him to get any more water so I had to use what I had. Standing in all of about two quarts of water, I began to bathe my soiled body. Water spilled onto the living room floor as I bathed.

The winter months were brutal when I stood in the living room bathing in the foot-tub. The freezing cold air blew in through the holes and cracks. Living in that shack was much like sleeping on the street corner because the structure provided little to no protection from the elements. While bathing in my foot-tub one winter night, I stood there bare and quivering. Beaten by winter's wind, I soaped my body with an old rag I used as a wash cloth. I credit those occurrences as contributing factors to the constant illnesses I suffered as a child.

It was getting dark, so I stepped out of the foot-tub after bathing and lit a couple of candles. I lay down in the bed and stared at the ceiling, which was covered with spider webs and black soot stains from all the candles and lamps I had burned over the years. I got out of bed when I heard Andrew's footsteps approaching. I opened the wooden lock that was nailed into the door frame serving as a door lock so Andrew could come inside. Andrew gave me a sandwich to eat and a cup of water. I thanked him before he left and I ate the sandwich in two or three bites. I said my prayers and lay back down to rest for the coming day. Midway through the night, I awoke because my stomach became upset from the egg sandwich. This was also another eye-opening experience I recall vividly. My toilet was more disgusting than the bathtub. There was only a little brownish water in the bowl that remained from when the shack had running water. The toilet's exterior was dingy; it had greenish-black stains inside and around its base. There was a large, rusty tin barrel filled with rain water behind the shack. I used the water from there to flush the toilet. I kept a plastic bucket next to the barrel to carry the water inside. When I used the toilet, I squatted and hovered over it, being careful not to touch it. I poured water into the toilet from the bucket, positioning the bucket high enough over the toilet to generate just the right amount of force to flush it. Sometime it worked, sometime it didn't, and when I was unsuccessful it would overflow onto the floor.

I kept my soiled bath water from my foot-tub to help flush the toilet. For a time it provided the additional water needed. The imagery from those years makes my stomach queasy. After playing the balancing act over the toilet in the unhealthiest conditions, I pondered for a better way, one that was more humane and less undomesticated. Therefore, I started going outside into the pasture (yards away from my shack) with the cattle to relieve myself. Most of the time, Madea wouldn't give me toilet paper, so I started using leaves and grass from the pasture to clean myself. On the days it rained or during late nights when I couldn't see well enough in the pasture, defecating in the middle of my living room was my alternative. I covered a portion of the floor with newspapers, squatted over it, and relieved myself. Afterwards, I folded the newspaper inside of other miscellaneous papers and discarded it. Because of it being too dark outside, I put my discarded waste inside the ceiling of the bathroom. For a while, I went back the next day and threw it out in the woods. Having a lamp was a high privilege for me because it took Madea nearly a year before she decided to let me use two of her kerosene lamps. I burned diesel in them because I was told kerosene cost too much. I was very excited to get the lamps because they illuminated my living room a lot better than the candles I had been using. It also made me feel almost like I had electricity. The downside of having the lamps was that whenever I ran out of diesel it would take a long time before Madea would allow Andrew to buy more. The shack was always the place I knew I could sleep in lieu of sleeping on the street, or at least that's what I thought.

There were many nights when I came home to the shack and there would be a lock on the door. I called out loud enough for Andrew to hear me from across the street. Andrew usually walked over and told me, "I'm sorry, Brad, but Madea don't want you to sleep in the shack tonight." I asked him once what her reason was for locking me out of the shack. He said, "You know how Madea hate you and Jackie, Brad, she hate y'all with a passion… You know that." Whenever this happened, I would sleep on the porch or outside in the pasture. There were many nights that I stayed on the street in Memphis, Glendale, and Cherry Hill, but refused to go to sleep like the other bums who slept on the corner. I would sit down on a bucket or whatever I could find and prop myself up against something and fight to stay awake. There were too many occasions when Madea did silly things, and locking the door to the shack was one of them.

Another occasion was when I came home after football practice heavily soiled. My body was gripped with dirt, mud clinging to my legs. I looked down in the corner near my bed where I kept my foot-tub, but couldn't find it. I continued to look for it throughout the house. Even though I normally didn't go into the other rooms, I desperately hoped to find it there. I continued searching for about a half hour and decided to give up. I thought to myself when I was searching, I *know Madea didn't bring her crazy ass over here and take my damn foot-tub.* I walked across the street and questioned Andrew. He hadn't seen it. Madea came outside when I was walking back across the street towards my shack and yelled, "Go buy your own damn foot-tub! Don't come over here bothering me about mine you ugly bastard."

Taking my tub was like taking a homeless man's grocery cart. That foot-tub was all I had to bathe in, and I was making the best of it. Much like the grocery cart of a homeless person, having it was essential. Madea really set the bar with that one. She had a knack for digging to lower depths each day. Andrew came across the street and gave me another foot-tub (a two-gallon foot bath) to bathe in. This one was even smaller than the one I had before. It was plastic and pink. He brought me some hot water to pour in it so I could bathe. This foot-tub disappeared later on that week, and my old aluminum one magically reappeared in the spot where I always kept it. I was happy to get my "premium" foot-tub back. Good grief!

There were times when Madea took my lamps and candles and hid them. Whenever she did this, I wouldn't have any light. I overcame this by simply learning to do without it. Andrew, acting as a mediator, convinced Madea to give him the lamps and he, in turn, gave them back to me. After that, sometimes I didn't light the lamps because I was so angry with how Madea was treating me. I thought that if I made her think I didn't need the lamps maybe she would stop taking them. I learned to cope with things like that while struggling to focus on school. In addition to this, Madea starved me most of the time by not allowing me to eat. During that time, Madea received a large sum of food stamps for my siblings and me. She received a monthly check from the government as supplemental welfare support for us, too. I struggled internally to become a better person and became more reluctant to sell dope. This also impacted me badly because I no longer had money to buy food when I was hungry. I remembered there was a blueberry orchard within walking distance. I learned of this one summer when several members of the football team and I got jobs there. We were hired to pick blueberries. Later on I started eating there. I remember many days giving away crack to some of the guys I hustled with. My brother, Charles, and older cousin, Maurice, were included in that number. I looked on as the remainder of my crack dissolved in the sun, outside of the shack. I was getting closer to getting out of the drug game completely. I sold crack off and on for a little while sparingly, and eventually stopped.

I continued selling marijuana because I realized it carried less jail time if convicted. I didn't make much cash selling weed because the profit margin was about forty percent. Crack can have a profit margin exceeding two hundred percent. I started Bible studies with some local Jehovah's Witnesses and learned about God. I told my mother about this one day during a visit, and she told me to make sure we read from the King James Bible and never to use their material. She said that there is only one God. I agreed and continued my studies with them from the King James Bible. I began to grow spiritually, and those studies shed light on how illiterate I was. I could hardly read well enough to complete a single sentence without pausing for one of the witnesses to sound out a word for me. This was due to my prolonged absenteeism and years of dropping out of school.

Coping with pain

❦

I started reading the Bible more on my own, and I became accustomed to living in the shack. I had begun to receive support from my relatives on the Hill. My cousin, Carl, and his lovely wife, Elizabeth, also pitched in. They welcomed me to eat whenever I was at their home. There were times when it was very apparent when I had worn out my welcome with family on the Hill. It took a lot to get to that point because I was practically living on the Hill at one time. There were many instances when Madea and Andrew were cooking and I smelled it from across the street. On one occasion, assuming I would be eating once the food was prepared, I would work out, lifting weights until it was dinner time. Once the food was done, Andrew would call me to come to the porch to get my plate. As he called me, Madea would be on the porch calling the dogs and cats to feed them leftovers. So we would all hurry to Madea's porch together, the dogs, cats, and I alongside them. To my surprise, Andrew handed me a plate of cold grits that had been cooked several days ago. The grits were from the same portion of food Madea was using to feed the cats and dogs. I looked at the plate and I looked at the dogs and cats eating the grits from the ground. I threw the plate onto the ground and told the dogs

144

and cats they had extras today. There were too many times when I ate the same thing as the stray dogs and cats. Normally I would have eaten those grits, as I did many days before, but this time I had another alternative. I walked about a half hour through the pasture to the blueberry orchard and ate blueberries. I was so hungry I didn't even pick or clean them. I ate them straight from the vine. I nearly choked on leaves and other foliage as I swallowed the hardly chewed blueberries. I ate all I could and walked back to my shack. My shirt, hands, and face were covered with blueberry particles and juices. I got some hot water from Andrew, poured it into my foot-tub, and soaped my body. After I finished bathing, I retired for the evening and fell fast asleep.

With a growling stomach awakening me in the middle of the night, I was perplexed. Stuffing my stomach with blueberries did little to cure my hunger, and I now regretted throwing away my grits. I observed a patch of blackberries that grew wild near a trash pile in front of my shack, and I ate from that blackberry patch. This was an everyday practice to prevent myself from starving. I grew weary of hoping and wondering if she was going to allow me to eat a meal. I didn't know if she was going to feed me the leftover scraps she set aside for the dogs or if anything at all. I became proactive and began to look around at my surroundings for things to eat. I realized that there was a pear tree in my backyard and a fig tree in Madea's backyard. On the days I was too exhausted from not having eaten to walk a half hour to the blueberry orchard, I would gather pears from the pear tree. On the days Madea was gone, I would sneak into her backyard and eat some of the figs from the fig tree. I had somewhat of a variety of things to choose from, although none of them would completely satisfy my hunger. But I was happy to have something to eat. That's how I normally ate during those years. I rotated between eating pears and blackberries that grew wild in my front yard. I indulged in endless raids of Mr. Coates's blueberry orchard, and the occasional figs I lifted from Madea's fig tree were tasty. I dreaded the slop Madea set aside for the stray dogs and cats. She divided it proportionately between the animals and me. Recalling a time when I hadn't eaten a meal in days, I saw Madea and Andrew on the porch with some day-old grits. Andrew called me over. I held back to the best of my ability from bursting into a full sprint. My counterparts weren't so patient. They all panted and ran towards the porch to eat the slop they were throwing on the ground for them. He gave me stale yellow grits to eat, but that time I ate them.

Playing football caused me to burn tons of energy, and that caused me to be hungrier than normal. This was another reason why playing football became burdensome to me. Once, before my first football game, the coach called us into the cafeteria to eat. I looked around at my teammates as we made our way to the cafeteria. I asked one of them how often we did this. He said we ate extra food before every game. I was praising the Lord silently as we entered the cafeteria. I sat down and ate more than all of the biggest boys on the team, including those who weighed over three hundred pounds. Whenever we traveled to an away game, we ate at Burger King after the game, and that was a big help for me. I needed to eat whenever and wherever I could.

When I was at Madea's house during one of her good spells, I noticed she kept a lot of coins in her bedroom in a dresser drawer. I started breaking into her house to steal those coins and walked to the Fast Mart to buy food to eat. I would stroll down to the store, planning in my head what I was going to buy. The store didn't have meat or produce. They mainly had canned goods and microwavable snacks. More often than not, I would buy two Little Debbie Zebra Cakes and a Fudge Rounds sandwich cake with the coins I stole. At times, I purchased honey buns and Vienna Sausages, and I always bought an ice-cold Dr. Pepper to wash it all down.

Once I purchased my snacks, I would hurry home as quickly as I could to eat them. I unknowingly purchased a few dollars' worth of snacks with some old, valuable coins probably worth several hundred dollars if sold to a collector or bank. Looking into the window of my past, I can see a young, innocent boy hurrying down the street to a shack he calls home to eat snacks bought with his grandmother's stolen coins. I can see that little boy sitting on a blanket next to his bed on the floor joyfully ripping open his snacks. He hadn't eaten in days, but he was abused daily. All he ever hoped for was love. He cracks his Dr. Pepper open halfway so that it will last longer and washes down the snacks he ate. He grins with a large smile upon has face and discards the empty wrappings. Brandon is bowing down on his knees and begins to pray. "Dear God, my father, bless me, I pray that I don't have to live like this forever. I pray, God that my life gets better. I thank you for the food I just ate, Father, in Jesus' name I pray. Amen."

When I first joined the football team, I quit several times because of many contributing hardships in my life. But once I learned the team was given extra food and ate at Burger King after away games, I played the entire year without quitting. I never ate at Burger King prior to going there after our away games. The first time I ate at Subway, was after practice and my friend Andre went there to get a sandwich on our way to bible study. He asked if I was coming inside with him after he parked his car. I sighed and looked at him and said "No man, I'm alright. I don't need anything to eat. I'll wait until I get home and eat then." Andre walked into Subway and stood in line, waiting to place his order. I looked at him and the other patrons inside selecting the toppings they wanted on their sandwiches. For some reason, Andre walked back outside and asked me to come in, offering to buy me something to eat. I laughed and insisted on staying in the car, and thanked him for being so generous. I can't remember Andre's exact words, but he said something to let me know that he knew I was hungry and I didn't have to be ashamed if I didn't have money to pay for my food. I walked into Subway with him and was deeply confused. I didn't know how to place my order. I embarrassed myself by standing in front of the line where people were paying for their food. Once I got in the right line, I was puzzled because I didn't know what toppings came on a Subway sandwich. I was concerned about being charged extra for the toppings, so I only asked for the toppings Andre got on his sandwich. That same day, I discovered I could have ordered as many toppings as I wanted, excluding extra meat or cheese, for no additional cost. I had a foot-long meatball marinara sub (my favorite sandwich there) with lettuce, tomatoes, jalapeno peppers and parmesan cheese. Mmm, that brings back some good memories.

One of my best memories while living in the abandoned shack is when my brother Charles and two of his friends, Mark and Shawn, came over to visit me. It was late in the evening and I was lying down in bed, but awake. I heard a car pull into my driveway. It was Charles and his friends carrying a bag full of beer. I was shocked because no one ever visited me; besides, I was too embarrassed for anyone to visit. They all walked in. "What's up man? What up nigga? Shit, just chilling," we said to one another. We gave fist pounds, smiled, and laughed while greeting one another. I started to get dressed after they sat down. I assumed they came to pick me up to go hang at their place. After I was dressed, they continued to talk, laugh, and drink beer. At that point, I realized they came to visit me, and I was subsequently happy. I lit all of my lamps and candles so they could have enough light. I spared no expense for those guys. I took good care of them. I even lit a few candles I had hidden in the event of Madea taking my lamps again. I moved my foot-tub to another room with a few other things so everyone could sit comfortably. We talked, drank, and laughed the night away. I can only assume that I was a good host because they all left cheerfully hours later. That was the first and only time I experienced anything like that. No one referred to the fact that we were in an old, abandoned house. No one complained about the horrible odor. No one commented or complained about sitting in a shack without lights or water. I followed them to the door as they exited, hoping the night would never end so they wouldn't have to leave. That was a moment when I felt normal, like everyone else.

The next day, I woke up and went to school. I tried my best to understand the things my teachers talked about in class. I had been dropping in and out of school for so long that I hadn't learned the basic material needed to understand high school coursework. One of my favorite times of the school day was when the school bell sounded and class was dismissed. I rode the bus to the Trap and got off there. I walked a few blocks to visit my mom at the women's jail. Before I went there, I gave some random guy cash to buy me a can of beer. He went into a corner store, bought the beer, and gave it to me. I bought two cans of Dr. Pepper and poured one of them out. I took the empty can and poured the beer into it. I bent the head of a sewing needle and used it to close the Dr. Pepper can. I poured some Dr. Pepper from the second can around the lip of the can that contained the beer, and I placed both cans in the same hand with the partially opened one on top. I pretended to drink out of it when I walked onto the jail grounds. The guards patted me down and causally glanced at the Dr. Pepper cans. I walked into the jail and waited for my mother to be summoned to the jail yard or visiting area. This was a surprise visit. She walked down and hugged and kissed me.

"My baby! My baby!" she said, "I miss you so much Brandon!"

"I miss you, too, Momma," I said, and gently passed her the can of Dr. Pepper.

She smiled and said, "You know I don't drink Dr. Pepper boy."

We walked outside into the jail yard and sat down at a wooden picnic table. This was the same table we always sat and played Spades or Dominos. I bought her a pack of cigarettes and some snacks from commissary. She pulled out a pack of cards and we started playing Spades. After some time, she finally got thirsty and opened the partially opened can of Dr. Pepper. My mother looked at me startled and said, "This can already open, Brandon."

I mirrored her surprised looked and said, "I know, Momma. Just drink it."

She placed the can to her mouth and reluctantly took a sip. While wearing a huge smile on her face, she said, "This ain't Dr. Pepper. This taste like beer." She was very surprised and inquired about how I got the beer in the can and resealed it so well. More than anything, she was happy to enjoy good tasting beer.

We began to play Spades and, later on, one of her friends joined in. I had a good time and I imagine my mother did, too. It was just like old times before mother got arrested. Mother was playing cards and drinking her beer. Once she finished the beer, she gave me the can and started to worry that the guards would smell the beer on her breath. I told her not to worry about that and passed her a can of Sardines. I bought them earlier to mask the odor of the alcohol. She ate the sardines and marveled at me. "Brandon, you are something else!" She looked at me with those bright eyes of hers; my mother was utterly amazed.

For her next visit, I offered to bring her some Mad Dog 20/20 or one of her favorite wines but she discouraged me from doing so and warned me that I could get arrested for bringing alcohol into the jail. After an hour or more had passed, our visit reached its end. We walked to the exit gate and hugged and kissed each other. Mother whispered that she loved me and I told her I loved her, too. I walked away from the jail compound and saw mother standing by the fence in the yard next to the roadway, as she usually did after a visit. She was smiling. I looked on at her and waved. I told her how much I anticipated our next visit. I told her I was going to invite Charles to play her and her cellmate in a game of Spades.

"Charles's ass can't play Spades," she said.

I walked around town until I saw my Uncle Andrew drive by and I motioned to get his attention. He looked over and saw me standing on the curb, wearing a ridiculous grin on my face. He pulled over to give me a ride. I got into the car and began to talk to him about my visit with Momma. I told him she was doing well, and that I was whipped horribly in a few hands of Spades by Momma and a couple ladies who were also serving time.

We arrived at Madea's house and I exited the car. I walked across the street to read the Bible as I told Mother I planned to do once I made it home. Now, here comes my little sisters and brother bolting into my shack from nowhere.

"Brad, how was Momma doing? Andrew told us you saw Momma."

"Calm down, now, before you give yourselves a heart attack!"

After I got them settled, I told them all about my visit with Mother, minus the beer incident. I told them our mother was building her body with lean muscle as she had done in previous incarcerations. They visited Mother as often as I did, but they always liked to gather around and listen to me tell stories about my visits with her. I formed a very strong bond with my siblings and they held me in the highest regard.

I dreaded the Christmas holiday and became very embarrassed every Christmas day. I absolutely hated my birthday. I never received anything for either occasion. Every Christmas, all my peers at school wore their new clothes or boasted about the gifts they had at home. I would stand there and pretend not to listen as they discussed their holiday gifts. Each year passed and I never received a thing. There were times when my mother would put together what money she had and buy us some gifts, which were received with great appreciation because they came from her. Madea and Andrew cooked a huge Christmas dinner every year. I thought I could look forward to Christmas dinner, but Madea stopped allowing me to eat Christmas dinner with them. The one time of the year I could go inside Madea's house and eat dinner with my brother and sisters had been taken away. My youngest sister, Star, boldly devised a plan for me to eat dinner one Christmas all by herself. She was only seven at the time. I'd never forget that Christmas evening when she came stumbling across the street, nearly falling down, carrying a big plate piled high with food and dessert. As I observed her walking, the first thing I thought was, *Christmas dinner? Could this be Christmas dinner?*

I received the plate from Star and thanked her. She smiled and ran back across the street without wasting any time. I thought for a second that Madea sent Star to give me the Christmas dinner. After a few hours passed, I found out Star had given me her Christmas dinner. Madea had threatened to starve Star if she ever gave me her food again. I lay in bed, happy to finally have a full stomach. I looked out my window across the street and listened for Star. I was a little worried about her and wanted to know that she was okay; I was afraid Madea might've beaten her or done something crazy. I lay back down across my bed and folded my hands behind my head. I thanked Star the next morning while walking to the bus stop, but I encouraged her not to do anything like that again.

There was another Christmas when Star surprised me a second time. It happened in almost the same manner as the first. I was lifting weights on the bench press in front of my shack and Star walked over. She told me she had something for me, so I threw the weights back onto the weight rack and leaned forward, asking, "What is it Star?"

She smiled and said, "I have a Christmas gift for you," and handed me a folded piece of paper. It read 'Happy X-Mas to my brother Brandon from your sister Star', written with green and red markers. I was happy and well pleased, but what she told me afterward made my heart melt even more. My little sister told me that she made me that gift because she knew I never got anything and she wanted me to have a gift, too — not to imply that she was showered with gifts. What little gifts (mostly charitable) she did receive were remarkably underwhelming. But at her young age, she didn't know the difference — or, at least, that's what I'd like to think. I got off the bench and hugged and thanked her. I held onto that piece of paper through the

by Brandon Williams

years and still have it today. That was one of the most thoughtful, kind gestures I received, by far.

I got along pretty well with Tricia and most of my family on The Hill. She supported and encouraged me to finish school, and also to play football. She always told me that I was special and that I had a story to tell. I liked Tricia very much, and speaking with her was a sort of therapy for me; she held a consistent roll in my life. But whenever I seemed to wear out my welcome, I would slack up on going to the Hill as often. No matter whose house I slept at, I always remembered that my old shack was my safe haven.

I started bonding with the guys on the football team, and that was my first time getting close with my peers at school since I was seven. I normally kept to myself as much as I could so no one would learn anything about my personal life. The coaches and my teammates started calling me "Brandon the Great" or "The Great One". I can't begin to explain how much I enjoyed hearing everyone chant those words. It started after a game I played well in. I had multiple sacks and many solo tackles. Most teams we played always had their guys double-team me. Usually, at nose guard and defensive tackle, I would defend against a guard or offensive tackle, but many times I would defend both. I used to sit in the back of the bus and rap whenever we traveled for an away game. That was a fun pastime most my teammates enjoyed. There would be someone beating on the seats and windows to make a beat. Someone beat boxed and another would sing the hook. "It's the mother fucking Brandon, Brandon, Brandon, Brandon, Brandon, Brandon," everyone shouted systematically. I would start rapping my heart out, saying anything that came to mind. Everyone noted me as being an excellent rapper, so I guess whatever I was doing worked. We normally rapped after our away games even if we were defeated.

School was getting a little better — it seemed being a part of the football team helped me cope. I became close to the teacher I was most afraid of, Ms. Phillips. She taught English and was known for giving scolding lectures to all the troubled students who didn't seem to care about getting an education. She referenced me as Mr. Williams, and she had a sweet voice. I was sitting in the classroom daydreaming one day and wasn't listening to what she was teaching.

"Mr. Williams, what do you think about that?" she asked me.

I was shocked because none of the other teachers bothered with me; they had written me off as a lost cause. Very few of them ever asked me questions in class. I corrected my slouched posture and leaned forward, trying to look as alert as I could. I replied, "Ma'am, can you repeat your question?"

Ms. Phillips said, "Hell, Mr. Williams, I repeated the question several times already, so why don't you go ahead and explain to the class your take on this matter?"

Everyone stared at me, fully aware that I didn't have a clue about what Ms. Phillips was asking. I continued to stare and raise my eyebrow as if I was pondering the hardest problem known to man. Ms. Phillips quickly grew tired of my stunt and told me that by the time I responded, we would all be dead and Glendale High would be closed down. She moved on to another student, who responded with the correct answer. Ms. Phillips asked me if that was the answer I was thinking of and I nodded my head. Of course she didn't believe me. The principal, Mr. Albert King, also became a very good support for me.

For the first time in my life, graduating high school became my goal, and it was within sight after being promoted to the eleventh grade. However, I reverted to selling crack on an off. I sold weed to some of my teammates, but I toned down my bad boy persona a lot. At one point, I slept in a different place almost every night, but now I spent most of my nights at my shack. There were times when I ate at Tricia's house and some of my younger relatives asked why. There were occasions when Tricia and her family looked on in astonishment as I ate. Those moments were the weirdest for me, causing me to become even more embarrassed about my life. I had to beg for food from almost everyone I knew. Tricia house was the main place where I ate during that time.

My late cousin Maurice would feed me at his house, and even told me I could live with him. One day, he and I were hanging around outside of his house because he didn't have his key. He asked if I had eaten anything. I shook my head. He would've fed me that day, as he did on a couple of other occasions, but we were locked out. I looked in his yard and saw some ripe watermelons growing. Maurice noticed me watching the watermelons and offered me one. I told him jokingly that since he insisted, I'd have one. I grabbed the biggest watermelon I could find and took a seat on the back of his truck.

"Well, are you going to eat it?" he asked.

I told him I didn't have any utensils to cut it open or eat it with. Maurice grabbed a watermelon, held it about waist high and dropped it onto the ground. It busted open perfectly into two halves. He picked up both halves of the watermelon and handed one over to me. After learning his technique, I must have burst open nearly a half dozen watermelons and ate them in the back of his truck. Maurice told me I could sleep overnight at his house whenever I didn't have a place to stay. I told him he should check with his parents first, in which he responded that they wouldn't notice me because they had so many people living there. I thought hard about Maurice's offer, but I never took him up on it because I didn't want to cause a problem.

I despairingly miss my cousin. He, as many of today's youth, was a victim of pointless violence. A guy gunned him down, but it isn't totally clear what actually happened. Some of my family members told me he had an argument with the baby daddy and estranged boyfriend of a woman he was dating. The guy and my cousin allegedly had a heated exchange of words one day at the woman's house. This resulted in my cousin pulling out his gun and firing in the direction of the guy as he ran for cover. I was told that my cousin didn't have any real intention on shooting the guy, but only wanted to scare him. The next day, the guy came back with a gun and murdered my cousin without argument at the woman's house. But nobody can really say what happened, other than those involved.

My success in football was realized when LSU head coach Gerry DiNardo came to watch me practice. I had started receiving mail from various colleges that were interested in recruiting me for their football programs. This was an "Aha!" moment for me because this contradicted everything my family had told me. How can someone as important as Gerry DiNardo take interest in me if I'm a "complete failure", as the Condescending Five proclaimed? I always knew they were ignorant people and I never really listened to their nonsense rhetoric, although I must say, most, if not all, of those malicious and hateful things they said hampered my confidence. I believed nothing good was supposed to happen to me. I only expected to experience momentary periods of happiness. I never expected much more than that for myself. I never realized how much they impacted my subconscious until years later. As I continued to progress in school and football, my self-esteem did, also. My bond with Ms. Phillips flourished and she became a lifelong confidante. She strongly encouraged me to complete school, and on one instance she gave me financial support.

For the longest time, I felt like my life was on autopilot, destined for destruction, and I didn't care. But now I know differently. It is quite profound the way emotion, self-esteem, love and self-value works, or the lack thereof affects us. I became more interested in the lovely young ladies of Glendale High, but shied away from them. I was too afraid to allow someone to grow close because they would discover my life as it really was. Therefore, I missed a lot of opportunities for companionship during my high school years.

I continued to visit my mother regularly. We spent many days in the yard of the jail playing Spades, laughing, and talking about the good old days. I established a few bonds with some of the women who were incarcerated with her. Meanwhile, the chaos that ensued living in my shack only got worse. Subpar living while trying to attain a high school education would be a difficult feat for anyone. The ridicule and verbal abuse from the Condescending Five worsened.

Several years earlier, my older cousin Daniel did something I'll never forget. He was in his twenties and I was thirteen. I hadn't started living in the shack yet; I was still living with Madea, Andrew, my grandfather and my siblings. Daniel came to Madea's house to borrow some money from her. He was in need because he had spent his on various women he courted outside of his marriage. Madea and I had an argument earlier that day and she was still upset about it. Daniel came in the house and I greeted him with a smile. He spoke to me and Andrew. Then Daniel stormed into Madea's bedroom and attempted to sweet talk her into giving him some money, as he had done many times. Madea refused to loan him the money and tried to send him away.

Before he left her room, she told him about the argument she and I had earlier. Daniel capitalized on the moment to change Madea's heart about giving him the money. He walked in front of me while I was sitting down and stood there for a moment with a blank stare. Without warning, he struck me in my face with his fist. The blow hurt my sense of being and value as a person more than it did physically. I looked up at him from my chair and a single tear of surprise rolled down the right side of my face. I considered trying to fight him back to defend myself, but I couldn't believe my cousin had done this. I openly admired and embraced him second only to my mother. He remained standing over me in the same position he was before he struck me. I can only assume he was about to strike me a second time before Andrew rushed over and grabbed him.

"Daniel... Daniel...Daniel...Stop...Stop!" Andrew screamed. "Don't hit Brad like that. He's a child!"

Daniel walked away.

Much like my abused mother, I wiped away the single tear that formed a stream from my swollen face. I was abused as a child, but I was afraid to tell anyone about it. I was ashamed and embarrassed. I felt like, somehow, it was my fault or that this sort of thing was supposed to happen to me. Madea walked into the living room, saw my bruised face and smiled. She looked at Daniel and invited him back into her bedroom. It was clear that Madea decided to give Daniel the money because he assaulted me, and expressing a strong sense of hatred for me had earned Daniel his reward.

There was another time that same year when James was about to attack me. I was in Andrew's bedroom watching television when James and his wife confronted me. James asked me to step outside so that he could assault me. I told him that I was standing right in front of him and asked why I had to go outside. He started to curse, yell, and hurl hurtful insults as I stood motionless. His wife stood behind him to lend her support, approving of her husband assaulting me. I began to pace the floor and said nothing while James shouted. I prepared myself mentally for the moment he struck so I could try to defend myself. After several minutes of making threats to harm me, James and his wife walked out of Andrew's room. She embraced him as they walked away as if he had done an honorable deed, as if he was a prized fighter being escorted from the ring. I sat down, nodded my head and sighed deeply, attempting to ignore the pain. My heart hurt. I was deeply grieved and tired of being everybody's punching bag.

My family was relentless in their physical and verbal abuse, but, after the age of sixteen, the physical abuse ceased and so did the threats. I suppose this was due to my change of attitude and body development. The neglect, as well as the mental and emotional abuse, continued, but at least I wasn't being beaten anymore.

At present day, many years later, my mother and I have somehow remained a topic of discussion. I was always aware of the fact that they hoped I failed in life and that my mother never got her life back on track. My younger cousin, Crystal, daughter of James, confirmed this for me one day. I received the most disturbing text from her asking why I hated her and my family, wondering if it was because of the abuse and hardships I suffered during my childhood. This text was random and I didn't have any idea where the origin of the topic developed, but the most telling part is that Crystal was only a small child during most of my sufferings. She was too young to understand what was going on in my life. I reasoned the Condescending Five were the origin of this text message discussion I was having with Crystal, who I love and embrace dearly.

I would like to share with you a story about an old man who hated his pet dog, Spunk. Spunk was very loving and protective of his master. Often, the old man rewarded Spunk's obedience with a swift kick in the butt. Then the old man would turn his back, laughing as Spunk hobbled away with his tail between his legs. The old man beat Spunk and starved him, too. Spunk was so malnourished that, although he was about two years old, he appeared to be a six-month-old pup. Despite the never-ending torture and ridicule Spunk received from his master, he loved the old man tirelessly. After many years of being beaten, starved, and emotionally abused, Spunk ran away. When the old man learned that Spunk ran away, he was deeply saddened and became very angry. He told all his neighbors that his good for nothing, ungrateful dog ran away. The old man grieved and was distraught. He told everyone in town how much he loved Spunk. Spunk received word of his master's outcries, so he decided to return home. Spunk, seeing his master seated on the porch, leaped into his lap only to be driven forcefully into the ground. The old man held Spunk down by thrusting his foot into Spunk's neck. He picked up a nearby branch and nearly beat Spunk to death with it. One day, a nice person passing by saw a battered and bloody Spunk and rescued him. He took Spunk away without the master's knowledge. The old man simply thought Spunk had run away again. The old man soon started spreading more rumors about how much Spunk hated him and ran away from home again. The truth is, Spunk never hated the old man. In fact, he loved him. The old man loved to hate Spunk and was saddened when he left because he had no one to torture and abuse. He hated Spunk even more for not being the subject of his abuse anymore. The abused dog depicted in this story is me and the old man is my family. The nice person who stopped and rescued me was Jesus Christ.

After several threads of text, I finally relented by telling my younger cousin I'd call her later to finish our discussion. She had a rebuttal for every effort I made in an attempt to reassure her that I did not hate her or my family. I'm not certain if someone put her up to this or if it came in light of hearing unfavorable discussions about me. Either way, her questions confirmed that, somewhere out there, the old man is still grieving because Spunk isn't around anymore. I love you, old man, and I'm sure Spunk loves you, too. I forgive you for hurting me and I have long released the grudges and distain I held for you during that time.

After many years of suffering from abuse, undernourishment, and homelessness, I had finally made it to the twelfth grade. It was a miracle — many of the people who knew my story told me so. "Brandon, you could've been murdered, killed someone, or in prison, but you still here," Tricia said. Tricia and Ms. Phillips really gave me a lot of confidence in my abilities and helped me discover my value within.

I shouted, "Yes!" repeatedly while holding the letter that said I was promoted to the twelfth grade. I realized more than ever that the possibility of completing high school was a very realistic one. By this time, I had completely stopped selling drugs, including the occasional marijuana I sold to my teammates. I continued shooting dice and gambling here and there to earn money. I was eating often at almost all of my friends' houses. I learned to rotate between them, being careful not to wear out my welcome as I did once before. I had long discovered going to school regularly was a guarantee I would eat at least twice that day. Not having food to eat wasn't much of an issue anymore, although a long day of football practice would deplete nearly every ounce of energy I had. But I enjoyed the extra meals I received even more because I was on the football team.

During my senior year, I developed a deep interest in Afro-American, American and world history. I read about Harriet Tubman and the Underground Railroad. Prior to this, I long held that the Underground Railroad was literally a secret passage underground that Tubman used to aid slaves to freedom. I read about it with a since of pride and enthusiasm for the countless white men and women, some of whom were abolitionists, that suffered, fought, and died to end slavery only to have their descendants (e.g. Freedom Riders) carry on their fight through equal rights protests and demonstrations alongside their black counterparts.

I registered to take the ACT test as my coach instructed me to. I had many prospective universities that were interested in recruiting me for an athletic scholarship, but they all cited that my grade point average of 1.87 was extremely low. Clark State University's coaches, Curt Wittman and Terry Jackson, were also interested. One day, I was called into the principal's office during my last school period. I walked into his office and was greeted by a proud Albert King. He asked me to have a seat and introduced me to Terry Jackson. I shook his hand, and he politely joked about possibly being my father. He told that joke because he and my mother dated back when they were in high school. Mr. King and Coach Jackson got straight to business by telling me that I should consider becoming a part of Clark State University's football program. When I asked about a scholarship, they explained that my grades were too low. They told me I could get financial aid until I improve academically and receive a scholarship afterward. I was happy to hear this news, and the thought of completing high school was received as a miracle. I couldn't imagine going to a university at that time. I thanked them both and Coach Jackson told me he hoped to see me in Midland soon.

I wasn't happy about getting letters and visits from various coaches without having a scholarship, but I really didn't understand the recruiting process. I thought my grades were bad but shouldn't be a factor on whether or not I received an athletic scholarship. I talked to Major Davison about this and he asked me if I had considered joining the Army. He told me that I was a great JROTC cadet and he felt I'd be a perfect match for the Army. I told him I thought about enlisting into the Marine Corps so I could adopt my younger siblings and become their legal guardian.

I spoke to my mother one day while visiting her in jail about adopting my siblings and she agreed. Madea cursed and was verbally abusive to them. She used to tell my sisters Jess and Star they were "onmless", which was one of the many words Madea invented or simply mispronounced. I believe this word is closely related to being a whore or prostitute. Jess was twelve, Star was nine, and Derrick was ten. Madea would regularly tell them they were onmless and that they weren't going to be shit, just like Jackie. They were three innocent little children subjected to this abuse. And since Momma was in jail, they had no one to take care of their hair maintenance needs. Madea used to tell my sisters that my younger cousin was better looking than them because she had a lighter complexion. Madea asked Lauren to perm Jess and Star's hair and to my surprise, she did. My sisters' hair was very long, but also thick and coarse because a while had passed since they had a relaxer. I remember both my sisters combing out huge locks of hair after Lauren relaxed it. They had burns around the edges of their hairlines and on the back of their necks. I was furious because I believed she purposely did that, as her and her daughter Crystal had extremely short hair — not to mention the fact that she hated my sisters. I told my sisters not to allow Lauren to touch their hair again. I felt so sorry for them and I offered to take care of their hair from that point on.

Days later, my sisters had lost almost half their hair. Their hair used to hang below their shoulders, and now it barely hung below their ears. I suppose Jess inquired about how to relax hair because I saw her relaxing Star's hair several months later. Madea offered to send them back to Lauren and they both declined, as I suggested. Jess started relaxing her own hair, too. Jess would try to comb and style their hair the best she could for a twelve-year-old. I started asking questions to various women about relaxing hair and learned quite a bit. I told my sisters that I would try my best to meet their hair care needs. Shortly after, I started relaxing, setting, washing, conditioning, cutting split ends, rolling, styling and giving them hot oil treatments in efforts to restore their hair to its original state. I was successful, and eventually their hair grew back as long as it had been once before. Their hair had sheen, bounce, and was very healthy. I was proud to see them happy with their hair again. As time progressed, my sisters started asking for more difficult hairstyles than I could do. I used to put in French rolls, buns, twists, ponytails, and braids. I decorated their hair age appropriately with borates, ribbons, scrunchies, hair clips, and pins as they requested. I used to style their hair according to the latest trend — or I tried desperately to, anyway. Eventually a classmate of mine that also was a daughter of one of Madea's friends started taking care of my sisters' hair.

I noticed on their birthdays, my siblings normally received a gift of some sort. It wouldn't be anything special, but at least they were getting something. Normally the gifts came from a local charity organization in Glendale, and sometimes from Momma or their fathers. We all had different fathers, though Jess and Star were rumored to have the same father. I never knew my father, but I met the man on three occasions. We met once when I was about six, a second time when I was thirteen, and the last time I saw him I was twenty-five.

I was mildly satisfied with the charitable gifts they received during the holidays and the underwhelming gifts they received from their parents. I noticed during the Easter holiday, the charity didn't pass out gifts so they usually ended up not celebrating the holiday. I started buying plastic Easter eggs and filled them with candy and dollar bills. I remember the first Easter I did that; my younger brother and sisters were in awe. They were surprised and joyful when I called them across the street to the compounds of my illustrious shack for an Easter egg hunt. I hid eggs filled with assorted candy and cash everywhere. I also bought my siblings chocolate bunnies and other festive items. I used the money I made from hustling in the trap to fund the Easter egg hunt. I was around fifteen or so at that time. I always found it amazing how much happiness doing a little wrong could bring your loved ones. Later that day, we had bible studies and I quizzed them on basic Bible stories afterward. I did this in keeping my mother's tradition. She always studied God's word with me and my older brother. I was more of a father figure to my siblings than a brother. In fact, my older brother, Charles, even admired and looked up to me because of my perseverance during the many struggles and hardships of my life. My siblings and I were very close, as we still are today.

by Brandon Williams

I struggled with alcohol during the latter part of my middle school years, as well as my freshman and sophomore years in high school. When I went to school after being on the street all night, I found it very hard to focus in class. All I would think about is the ridicule I would face if someone found out I was homeless. I was insecure about the state of my life and with who I was. I hated myself, I hated being poor, and I detested being hated by my family and everyone else. I was so discontent with myself that I was suicidal. Going to school filled with classrooms of happy children saddened me because I was forced to become an adult at thirteen. I never had the luxury of not worrying and just being a kid. I was introduced to the street life at the young age of seven and became a gun-packing certified hustler (gangster) by the age of thirteen. I grew up very quickly, living the street life or what some would call a 'thug's life', but I always wanted to be the kid I really was. Going to school only reminded me of how different my life was from the other kids. So I started drinking Night Train, MD 20/20, and White Port every morning before I went to school. "No pain, no worries," I used to say while tilting my head back to take a sip. Alcohol consumption before going to school was my way of coping with daily stress. I used to get drunk almost every morning before school.

Once I had alcohol in my system, I didn't worry about what the other kids had or what I didn't have. I didn't care because I was high and feeling good. The days I went to school intoxicated, I normally would be more social with everyone and I laughed at everything. I often skipped class and shot dice with a couple guys. Depending on who my teacher was, I shot dice in the back of the classroom while he or she discussed our assignment for the day. I sat in the back of the classroom and had a student in front of me to distract the teacher while I gambled. If I won, I paid the student a small fee, and if the other person won, he paid. There was something in it for all of us and that's how I influenced others to participate. Needless to say, there always was that stubborn kid in school who had the perfect life but 'wanted to be down'. I pitied kids like that and didn't associate with them very much unless I was scolding them and telling them how they need to be true to themselves and thankful for their good lives.

Life was hard, but my mother and I made the best of it. There was a period in my youth when I bathed and washed my face with bleach. I tried to bleach my skin many times over, desperately hoping to attain a lighter complexion. This came about after being told repeatedly I was too black and too ugly. I walked with a slumped over posture intentionally, hoping not to appear as tall as I was. I began to do so after I was told regularly that I resembled a big, black gorilla. I used to dream about grafting hair from the back of my head to the front of my scalp. This was something I vowed to do once I had enough money because of the taunts I received about having a big head. All of the complexes I developed regarding my appearance and intellectual ability were a direct result of the verbal and physical abuse I received as a child.

Marine Corps

With the last-minute cramming and stress of final exams behind me, I eagerly awaited my test scores. I received passing grades in all of my classes for the first time. My twelfth-grade year was my best year in school; I didn't sell drugs, I wasn't violent, and I completed the whole year without prolonged absences or dropping out. I must credit most of my success to my cousin Daniel and his lovely wife Erica. They allowed me to live with them during that time. I also lived with them briefly during my seventh-grade year. This was my first time since I was seven that I had stability in my life. Despite Daniel abusing me when I was younger, I felt he cared for me more than anyone else in my family, excluding my mother. Although I didn't feel totally secure because I lived from house to house for the majority of my life, living with Daniel was no different. I was fully aware that he and his wife had no obligation to me. Living with them did earn me the rite of passage to be an "average" youth. Bathing in a bathtub or taking a shower rather than standing in a small foot-tub in several quarts of water was an overwhelming change. Life was less complicated; I ate three meals a day, and sometimes more. As Daniel would have it, I ate without ceasing. I didn't have to worry about Madea snatching a plate of food out of my hand. I no longer had to rely on eating wild berries, blueberries, or figs to keep from starving. I enjoyed sitting down on a toilet in a sanitary bathroom. It was a far cry from stooping over in the woods, hovering over newspaper in my living room, or playing the balancing act when I initially attempted to use the filthy toilet in my shack.

I was elated about the fact that I was able to eat daily rather than not knowing where my next meal would come from. I was finally enjoying the bare necessities of life that I once held as an inconceivable privilege. I became a miracle in the eyes of many that knew the horrors of my life. I was highly esteemed and greatly celebrated by a select few. My mother, Tricia, and Ms. Phillips were the chief principles in all of my emotional support.

My high school administration planned a cruise to the Bahamas as a senior trip for my graduating class. The administrators also brought in vendors for us to order our cap and gown for graduation. A class ring could be purchased also, and most students bought one. Times were tight for Daniel and Erica and they were not able to assist me in paying for any of those items. I was deeply saddened when I visualized myself walking the aisle to accept my diploma without wearing a cap or gown. "What an embarrassment," I thought to myself, but shortly afterward I was just fine. Graduating for me was more than enough; no one thought I would complete high school, including most of my family, teachers and administration. I'm not sure who gave me the money to pay for my cap and gown. But if memory serves me correctly, it was Ms. Phillips. Now I no longer had to worry about that, but what about that trip to the Bahamas?

I knew that taking a cruise to the Bahamas was impossible. "How ridiculous," I said, although I wanted to go as badly as anybody else. Unbeknownst to me, Elizabeth, the mother of my good friend, Brian, had given him the money to sponsor my cruise to the Bahamas. I know this may sound cliché but words can't express how happy I was when I found out that I would be going to the Bahamas with my classmates. Yet another issue arose even after my trip was paid for. One of my teacher chaperones told us we would be stopping in Orlando, Florida. They told us this stop wasn't covered by the cruise fee and we needed to bring money with us for food and shopping. Most of my classmates were happy to hear this, but I hated learning of this. I wrestled with the idea of how to avoid being embarrassed in Florida. How would I tell my classmates and teammates that I wasn't hungry or I wasn't interested in going inside Universal Studios? At the very last minute, somehow, my mother and one of her cellmates at the jail came up with more than $300 for my trip. I had as much money, if not more, than all my classmates. For the first time, I felt I was on even ground with everyone else. I went to school the day of my trip full of excitement and anxiety. When we started to board the bus, my cousin Tricia drove up and called me to her car. I walked over to her vehicle and said hello.

She reached into her purse and handed me a wad of cash. She told me it was for my trip and she didn't want me to travel without any money. I told her my mother and one of her friends in jail had given me $300. But Tricia insisted on me keeping the money anyway and suggested that I used it for extra spending cash if needed. I thanked her right after I hugged and kissed her. I balled up the cash and stuffed it into my pocket as I boarded the bus. I had about $500 with all of the money combined.

Once we arrived in Orlando, all the students started pulling out their cash to show off and I sat there quietly while they did this. Everyone asked a particular student whose parents normally gave the best of everything how much money he had. He told them he had about $300, and out of them he had the most money. I felt even more blissful upon discovering that the least of them has been exalted. We had a blast in Orlando! We luckily stumbled across a free Tyrese concert. We rode many of the rides in the amusement park and I ate whatever I wanted. For the first time, price didn't matter and that felt good. Most of us went shopping and I bought a pair of nice tennis shoes. They were a pair of tan colored Reeboks. This was the first pair of shoes I bought that wasn't paid for with welfare or drug money in nearly four years. We stayed overnight in Orlando in a nice hotel. The next morning, I woke up and dove into the swimming pool minutes before we boarded the ship to cruise to the Bahamas. A few of my teammates opened their windows and looked on at me.

"Is the water cold?" one of them asked as the others stood by, waiting for an answer; to which I replied cheerfully, "No!" Moments later, they all bombarded the pool.

Cruising to the Bahamas was amazing. The sound of a roaring ocean arrested my attention and the deep blue waters were more captivating than anything I'd ever seen. Once we docked, I went into a store that sold memorabilia and exchanged a few bucks of US currency for some Bahamas dollar bills. I saw so many beautiful women from many different nationalities. I nearly lost my virginity in the Bahamas with another tourist. I don't remember her name, but she was from Lebanon. She had a beautiful physique paired with long, black hair. It glistened as the rays of heaven reflected off of it. She wore a black, two-piece bikini and her fingernails were painted black. Her skin was flawless and she was all together lovely. She had big oval shaped eyes that drew me into a trance. Her beauty conquered me and I was helpless. I abandoned all of my classmates and enjoyed deep conversations with her for what felt like hours. She stared at me and followed me as I treaded the water in the swimming pool. She asked me what my name was and where I was from. She also asked, "Why do you sound like that?"

"Like what?" I asked.

She responded, "Like a country white person."

I chuckled lightly. "No I don't." I thought I sounded like me.

She swam close to me and held my hand and told me that my accent was cute. After a lengthy exchange of flattery, it was quite apparent that the young lady was interested in having more than a conversation. Being the fine Southern gentleman I am, I asked her about her relationship with God. In the most foolish way, I reasoned that if I had sex with this woman she better have a relationship with the Lord. She told me the startling truth, which was that she didn't believe in God. I looked at her in awe and repeated her words to make sure I heard her correctly. "So, you telling me, you don't believe in God?" Upon learning this about the lovely lady, I finally gave in to the continual, "Come on Brandon, we're waiting for you," from a couple of my classmates. I hugged her one last time and ended our conversation. I walked away with my friends and turned to look at her one last time as she swam. She watched me, also, as I walked away. One can fairly say that requiring someone to be a Christian before being intimate with him or her is a questionable and contradictory practice.

My classmates and I enjoyed the beautiful views and scenery of the island. I walked to the beach with a couple of friends and dove into the ocean. A couple local women asked to take a picture of us. We swam back to shore and posed for the ladies as they snapped pictures of us as if they were the paparazzi. The day quickly dwindled to its end and we boarded our ship. Seeing the sunset over the ocean was a breathtaking sight, the sun rays bouncing across the sparkling deep blue. When we arrived back in Glendale, I was exhausted. I had taken a picture aboard the cruise ship to give to my momma during my next visit.

I returned to school the next day for graduation rehearsal. My mother wrote a letter to the warden requesting to be allowed to attend my graduation. We received word a couple days before graduation that her request had been denied. I was deeply saddened, but Mother reassured me things would be okay. She stood there in the compound of the jail, leaning against the fence, and I listened as she spoke. "Brandon, I'm so proud of you. You came a long way…and I love you." She asked me to stop by the jail before I went to my graduation so she could see me. I agreed, smiled, and told her I loved her, too.

On the day of graduation, Charles and one of our cousins picked me up. Charles and my cousin were smoking a blunt (cigar emptied of tobacco and refilled with marijuana).

"What is that smell? Man, y'all going to have me smelling like weed."

They laughed as if I had told a prize-winning joke of the day. Charles offered me the blunt and I told him no thanks. I was known for selling weed and many other drugs, but I wasn't much of a user. They kept pressuring me, and by that point I was already high from the contact smoke. They rolled the windows up and told me I was getting high that day, one way or another. My cousin blew me a charge, which meant he blew smoke directly into my nostrils as I inhaled. I coughed, my eyes watered, and I began to feel enlightened. Weed affects everyone in different ways. For me, it made me more talkative. I would become the greatest philosopher in an instant after only a few puffs of marijuana. About nine or ten charges later, I was high as a space shuttle. My eyes were bloodshot, red, and hazy. My breath reeked of alcohol because I had been drinking forty ounces of Olde English 800 malt liquor all day.

My Marine Corps recruiter called me on the cell phone he had given me several weeks prior. I straightened up my shirt before answering it as if he could see me through the phone. Sgt. Kelly wanted us to meet him at a corner store so he could drive me to the graduation. My brother and cousin laughed because I was high and I smelled like alcohol and weed. I was about to get into a vehicle with a recruiter from the United States Marine Corps in that condition.

I got out of their car and mistakenly left behind my tassel. I sprayed lots of cologne over myself to mask the scent of weed. Sgt. Kelly and I drove to the jail to visit my Momma. We stood by a fence near the jail yard and waited for her to walk over. She ran to the fence with bright, beaming eyes and congratulated me. She handed me a card through the fence that she and another inmate had crafted themselves. The enclosed caption read, 'Brandon, I know you are a man now but when I see you, all I see is my baby. I love you very much.' I introduced Sgt. Kelly to my mother and they politely greeted one another.

by Brandon Williams

"Take care of my baby," she warned him sternly.

"I will, Ms. Jackie," he told her to offer reassurance that my decision to join the United States Marine Corps was a good one.

We ended our conversation by saying, "I love you," to one another, as we normally did.

The recruiter and I drove to my high school. Once we arrived, I realized I looked a little different than my classmates. They were dressed in black gowns, orange tassels and black caps. I had everything except my tassel. I left it behind in my brother's car earlier. Our graduating class got in line and Principal King was about to begin commencement. I was so high and intoxicated; I could hardly stand steady in line. When my named was called to receive my diploma, it was a dulled moment. I was miserably drunk and didn't even smile; I was focused on not falling down and embarrassing myself. And I was a bit disappointed with the fact that the warden wouldn't allow my mother to attend. The jail she was in was located roughly ten miles away from my high school. I wanted to slap that warden in his face for failing to be fair and impartial.

This was it — I had finally graduated amidst the popular belief that I wouldn't. I rejoiced and thanked God repeatedly. My journey to completing school was a long one. Failing the fourth grade twice, dropping out of middle school twice, and nearly dropping out a third and final time in the ninth grade. A few weeks had passed since graduation, and it was time for USMC basic training. I was very pleased to be a part of "The Few. The Proud. The Marines." I hadn't picked a military occupation specialty (MOS) yet because my recruiter advised that more jobs would open once I started basic training. I was excited to be a part of something and have a sense of belonging. Unlike most of my life, for the first time, I was no longer a homeless youth searching for his way. The day of my departure for USMC basic training camp, I visited my mother at the jail. We ate lunch, prayed, laughed, and prayed more. My mother was proud of my decision and happy to see me off the street, but she was also concerned about my safety in event of a war. My mother and I had discussed me taking full custody of my three younger siblings Jess, Star, and Derrick. She agreed that once I completed basic training, I could take custody.

My Uncle Andrew drove me to the airport in Memphis. I hugged him and told him I loved him once we arrived. He wished me well and drove away. I was embarking on yet another challenge, going to an unfamiliar place filled with people I didn't know. This was a huge leap for a young, underprivileged teen from the rural South.

This was my first time flying. In fact, it was my first time leaving Tennessee, not counting my senior trip. I had mixed feelings about it all. I was excited and I felt a little lonesome at the same time. I boarded my flight and began to pray for a safe flight and for God to protect my mother and siblings. The captain said that we may experience some turbulence during our flight to San Diego, California. I had no idea what turbulence was and I was too embarrassed to ask anybody what it meant. After experiencing what felt like a compact car driving on a roadway filled with small potholes, I quickly concluded that this was the turbulence the captain warned us about. He announced after a few hours in the air that we would be landing at San Diego International Airport. I looked out of the window and embraced California with a smile. I exited the plane and walked through the terminal, looking for the Marine Corps official my recruiter said would be waiting for me and the other recruits. I saw a large group of recruits standing together near an exit, chatting amongst themselves. They had formed a circle and a few of them wore smirks on their faces with their chests poked out.

"The Few, the Proud, the Marines," I said with sarcasm as I greeted each of them.

"Why does he talk like that?" one recruit said to another. Then another recruit quickly intervened by telling the other two to mind their business. "This man here is from the south. My mother says nothing but good people come from the south. Now isn't that right? What's your name again?"

"Brandon, my name is Brandon and yes, your mother is right. Everyone knows the south is filled with God-fearing Christians who are unburdened with wrong doing." All of them looked at me with a blank stare. They didn't know if I was serious or joking.

"There they are," said one of the Marines who had come to escort us to Camp Pendleton. They ushered us to the airport parking lot where a chartered bus awaited. There was a moment of extreme silence after we boarded the bus. I wondered if the entire basic training was going to be this quiet. Within a few minutes, several drill sergeants blitzed the bus, shouting orders. They gave orders with the expectation of causing confusion and evoking fear. Each drill instructor gave contradictory instructions. One boarded the bus yelling, "Attention! On your feet, women. Why in the hell are you still seated?"

"Sit the fuck down... Sit the fuck down maggots!" another instructor shouted. This sort of drill continued for several minutes. I looked at the other recruits and every one of them was visibly shaken. I, on the other hand, was deeply amused at the instructors' attempt to be gritty.

The instructors gave us blindfolds and instructed us to put them on. Once we had the blindfolds on, the instructors inspected us to make sure we wore them properly and couldn't see. Shortly afterwards, we departed the airport for Camp Pendleton. I heard someone crying along the way and a drill instructor offering to throw him off the bus if he didn't stop. I tried to trace every turn and count every stop we made as we traveled. At one point, it seemed like the driver was driving in circles. The bus made a final stop and the drill sergeants ordered us to take off the blindfolds. It was around four or five o'clock in the evening when we arrived at the camp.

The basic training camp looked similar to a university campus with large patches of sand scattered around. It took a while for me to get used to the humidity.

"Who in the hell asked you to put those blindfolds on?" a master sergeant asked with the instructors who ordered us to wear them standing in the background. "Surely not one of these fine gentlemen, did they? You over there, who told you to put on the blindfold?" The recruit answered that he didn't know. "You are fucking lying. Who let this God damn liar into the United States Marine Corps?"

"Faces in the dirt," was one of the first orders I could remember receiving at Camp Pendleton. We all hopped off the bus and dropped to the ground unilaterally, faces planted in the dirt, and waited for our next command. A drill instructor yelled, "On your feet!" and we jumped to our feet. Then we were escorted to a medical clinic to get a series of shots. I have no earthly idea what types of shots we got; all I remember is being sore wherever the needle struck me. I sat on my left butt cheek for several hours while waiting to get the remainder of my shots because the right one was too sore. In the clinic, I saw hundreds, if not thousands, of recruits who arrived sometime the same day. We came from many different parts of the country, but we all shared the same goal: Protect the nation we love. We remained in the clinic until 3:00 AM the next morning. A drill instructor came over and gave those of us who had received a certain number of shots permission to go to sleep. He told the others to get rested once they were done. I fell into a deep sleep and dreamed I was still in Glendale until recruits woke me as they passed to get their shots. I dozed off again to be awakened this time by a drill sergeant who escorted us to our barracks. There, we stood at attention by our bunks and waited to be issued our gear. We were also told that we would meet the "Senior" (senior drill instructor). We were issued several jogging suits with the USMC anchor and globe embroidered on them. We received one pair of sneakers that were referred to as "go fasters". We were given a shaving kit, soap, and other hygienic essentials. We stored all of these items in a chest located at the foot of our bunks.

The Senior entered the room and the drill instructor ordered everyone back to attention. "At ease," the Senior said as he walked passed without making eye contact. The Senior spoke to us individually and as a group. He looked at my ASVEB score and told me that I scored high enough to join the Air Force and asked why I joined the Marines? I told him that the Marine Corps seemed to be more reputable and I cited how much I loved the blood-striped trousers. He smiled for a tenth of a second and said, "Now that's a true jarhead."

I told him I also joined the USMC so that I can adopt my younger siblings.

"Very impressive," he said. "And where are your parents?"

"I never knew my dad, and my mother is in jail, Sir."

"Well then, seems like you made the right choice. Welcome to the Corps, son."

We moved into formation and marched outside to see where everyone was with marching and basic military life. When I enlisted in the Corps, I entered as an E-2 Private-First Class because of the two years I served in JROTC. Many of my peers were E-1 Privates. There was an average of fifty people in a platoon, and there were about 20 different platoons that I saw training concurrently. The drill sergeant ordered us to form a single file column; in layman's terms, that translates to forming one line.

"At the sound of my command, I want you all to dress right dress," and he had other drill instructors demonstrating what this meant. To "dress right dress", we extended our left arm towards the right shoulder of the person standing next to us, to form an equal space between each of us. The drill instructors put us at ease and yelled because many of us didn't execute the command correctly. One of the instructors called another E-2 out of formation to demonstrate. He did so with excellence, so the drill instructor began to give him other commands that had not been shown yet and he demonstrated those as well. "Great job, leather neck. You are hereby pronounced our platoon leader. How do you like your new job, maggot?"

"Good, Sir. I love my job, Sir," he said with enthusiasm.

We continued a series of drills for the rest of the day and days following. We skipped lunch because so many people made mistakes, but we all ate dinner. As punishment, the instructors told us we would eat, shower, and shave "by the numbers". I didn't know what this meant until we walked into the mess hall and I heard other instructors counting aloud as recruits from other platoons ate. "Thirty-one thousand … You're done! Get up … Move … Move … Now!" and they had hardly dug into their dinner. I imagine they were some well-to-do lads eating with utensils and properly cutting their meats. I, on the other hand, ate by the numbers all my life. That is, if I ate anything at all. When it was our platoons turn to eat, I got my tray and before the last person sat at my table to eat, I was already done.

"What the fuck happened to your tray, maggot? Did you give your food away?"

"No, Sir!" I answered the drill instructor. "I ate it, Sir," I exclaimed loudly.

He walked close enough to me and put his lips in my ear. Whispering softly, he asked, "Do you know what?"

"No, Sir, I didn't give away my tray, Sir." Then he began to scream in my ear at the top of his voice, "Now don't let that happen a-fucking-gain, you fucking cunt!" Meanwhile, one of our instructors arrived at thirty-one thousand, which was our stop time. We emptied our trays and got back into formation and marched to our barracks. I admired the hot shot that instantly won the favor of the drill instructors and became our platoon leader. I wished it were me. I could do all of the things he did. I believed I could've easily executed every command as he did. Little did I know, time would soon show the drill instructors my knowledge and skill.

We were marching to our barracks once and our platoon leader made a mistake that led the entire platoon into the middle of another platoon's formation. After the drill instructors from both platoons finished yelling at him, I felt sorry for our platoon leader. Faces in the dirt, our instructors said, "One for all and all for one, you will pay the price. Get up and double knot your go fasters (shoes); we're going to do a little PT." He ran us senseless. We were coughing and spitting up mucous. A few passed out and were taken to the infirmary. Some stopped running and walked until they got yelled at by other drill instructors that appeared from nowhere. After a rigorous three-mile, uphill run, we got into formation and marched back to the barracks. The instructor had chosen the fastest guy during our run to be our new platoon leader. The guy looked like Vin Diesel's double with twice the muscle.

We marched to our barracks without any hiccups and started showering. After I finished, I got in line to shave. I didn't have a single strand of facial hair but the drill instructors insisted that everyone shave. One of them stood behind those of us that were shaving and started counting. "One thousand and ten; put down your razors." He walked over to each of us and inspected our faces. "Dismissed," he said dreadfully after he discovered not a single one of us had any facial hair remaining after we shaved. We got into our bunks and were told to rest up for the long day that awaited us tomorrow.

We marched and performed various drills nonstop throughout the following morning. A certain drill instructor tried to single me out as he did to everyone within my platoon. He looked down at me and asked, "Who are you?" I told him my name and he replied, "That's not your name, son. Your name is Recruit. Do you understand?"

"Sir, yes Sir, my name is Recruit, Sir!"

A couple of other drill instructors joined in. "Are you smiling, son?" Another said, "I'll wipe that silly smirk off your face," as he approached me nearly nose-to-nose.

I found it humorous that these well-groomed instructors tried to intimidate me. The more they yelled and shouted, the more they provoked me to laugh. Thank God I restrained myself. I held it in. I assumed they weren't going to shut up unless I appeared to be shaken by their antics. Therefore, I pretended to be nervous in hopes of shutting them up. It worked, and they all backed away like a pack of wolves, continuing the drills.

The next morning was uniform inspection. We were dressed in our BDU's and commando boots. My boots were polished to perfection and I wore my uniform perfectly, just as I did when I was in JROTC. The drill instructors didn't find anything wrong with my uniform, but they had many questions about my tattoos. When asked, I told them "Brad" was my nickname and the acronyms "LIVE" stood for Living 4 Eternity.

"How patriotic," the instructor said and walked away, exclaiming how ugly my tattoos were. As the days grew into weeks, I noticed a couple of instructors watching me. They would stand at a distance and stare in my direction as they talked amongst themselves. "You ... You there, you will be our new platoon leader. That other guy doesn't know what the hell he's doing." With my eyes fixed on my drill instructors, I tried to decipher if they were really talking to me. "Are you deaf? Get over here and take them to chow now ... Move, maggot."

"Platoon, attention," I commanded hesitantly. "Forward," brief pause, "*March*," to the mess hall we marched. I was shocked that the instructor chose me. Although I considered myself a standout recruit, I didn't expect anyone else did. The drill instructors marched alongside me, calling cadence. Your left, your left, your left right, we marched to his cadence and yelled, "Delta company!" at the end of each cadence. We ate chow and reported to our barracks for hygiene.

The drill instructors gave us ink sticks (ink pens), information on the history of the Corps and lectured us on it. Once they concluded the lecture, they ordered us to get well rested for tomorrow. I was told by one of the instructors that I was doing a great job. It was highly unusual for me because no one ever told me I was doing well. One of the drill instructors punished me because a few recruits in my platoon were off step and the instructor said that embarrassed him.

"On your faces, in the dirt!" I dropped down and put my nose in the dirt. My body was parallel to the ground in a pushup position. He stood over me and shouted, "Up, down!" He did this until my arms were shaking and it was apparent I wasn't physically capable of doing anymore pushups. "Up, down…On your feet!" This motivated me to take a stronger position as a leader and take command of my platoon as the instructors did. Once I took that approach, I won instant notoriety from many of the drill instructors, but I also inherited more criticism from others. I remember, one day, I was leading a small squad of six or seven men, and I saw a Lieutenant approaching. Whenever military personnel see a superior officer, they are supposed to salute them and, in turn, the officer will say, "As you were," signifying for the subordinate to continue as he or she was before. My men and I stopped and saluted the officer. We waited for him to say, "As you were," but he never did. He kept walking. I saw the same officer get saluted by a group of white recruits and he told them to carry on as they were, and they went on about their business. This happened periodically during basic training. There was a time when I was walking to the infirmary and I stopped to salute two white officers. Both walked past me without acknowledgement and one whispered something to the other and they started laughing. At that point, I put myself at ease and continued walking to the infirmary. I began to question the character of certain officers. I continued successfully as the platoon leader and won the respect of many of my peers, minus those who envied me because they wanted to be the platoon leader.

Released from Duty

We neared our second month of basic training and each platoon lost about half of their recruit's. Some were kicked out and others attempted suicide. I was flabbergasted that someone would try to take their life because of the pressure of basic training. Some got injured during training and were sent home for medical reasons. We had a few gay recruits that were sent home. The best I could understand, those that pretended to be gay and the handful that pretended to be suicidal never got sent home. Their actions only earned them a longer stay at the USMC basic training. As the weeks progressed, training became more intense and so did the drill instructors' expectations of us. I guess that coupled with fear and anxiety caused a lot of recruits to look for a way out. There was this one guy that tried to get discharged by pretending to be suicidal. He jumped out of a window of a two-story building and landed in a pile of sand. He sustained little to no injury; no more than the couple of minor scratches or abrasions. He was sent to the psych ward to be evaluated and was cleared to continue training. "He should've tried harder," one of the drill instructors said. "If he doesn't want the Marines, then the Marines don't want him."

I heard rumors of a couple of guys pretending to be gay. They were supposedly kissing each other in attempts to get thrown out the Corps. I witnessed a group of recruits, one day, in the chow hall, flamboyantly strutting and twisting their hips as they marched in formation. I'm not positive if anything ever became of this incident. But I continued about my business and kept a clear head. I was happy to be there. Being in the Corps was a way to provide a better life for myself and my siblings. The drills and marching became intense, and I discovered there was much more to marching than I had originally thought. I learned the true meaning of a cadence call, also. While in JROTC, I learned a series of commands and how to execute multiple steps with regard to marching. Hearing my JROTC peers and instructors call cadence meant nothing more than keeping in sync with the platoon. In the Marines, marching and battle marching while carrying a high-power assault rifle meant something different. It meant that we were being prepared to carry the weight of the nation on our shoulders whenever called into action.

I was taught how to think, which was to kill efficiently and be fearless while doing so. The instructors taught us what it meant to be the first line of defense. It meant we subjected our bodies to severe brutality and pushed ourselves to the limit each and every day. "Country before man," as some would say. "If you don't fight out here, if you don't have heart here, you won't in battle." Being regarded as the best meant we had to also be respected as the best trained and we were.

Cadence calling wasn't only a call; it soothed our spirits whenever we got weary or depressed. It was like the drill instructor was singing melodies to our soul every time he called cadence. Although I've never been in a war abroad, I can only assume the way cadence impacts the thousands of troops who have been called to duty.

It was now time to get our MOS and we reported to the main office to receive that information. Everyone became excited and asked each other what job they chose. When this question was directed to me, I simply stated I hadn't chosen a job yet. I explained that my recruiter told me to wait until basic training started before I chose a job because more jobs would be available. Some wished their recruiters would've told them that and others said I was misled. Another peer and I had a harsh exchange of words when he told me the Corps ultimately placed everyone in infantry if they enlisted without selecting a MOS.

Later that day, I discovered he was right. I was given the job of grunt (03). I, for the first time during training, was broken and deeply saddened. I refused to accept my duties and insisted that my recruiter had deceived me. He had lied, telling me I could pick my MOS once I enlisted. The senior drill instructor asked me for my recruiter's name so he could question him about the matter. He called down to the recruiting office in Memphis to address this matter with my recruiter, Sergeant Kelly. The Senior put down the phone and told me Sgt. Kelly wasn't working out of the Memphis office anymore. He had recently been promoted.

"Promoted?" I lamented with disgust. "I imagine he's out there lying to every potential Marine that walks into his office."

The Senior sympathized, but insisted I pulled myself together and get past this moment. "If not for yourself, do it for your family," he told me.

"I don't know what to do, Senior. I can't continue my life a lie. I don't want this job. This is not what I signed up for."

"Son, you don't have a choice. Besides you're the best damn Marine that came into my office in a long damn time. I know that you will make one hell of a Marine. You will do our country some good. You are a natural born leader. Just look at how well you have been doing here despite where you came from. Think about how much respect you've gained from your peers as platoon leader. Son, I suggest that you suck it up and deal with it. Worst things worst, you will be a grunt for two years and then you will be eligible to make a request for a new position."

"Two years?" I asked the Senior. "I have to be in infantry for two years based off a lie my recruiter told me?" I burst into tears and said I failed my family because I would not continue my training.

"You signed a four-year active, two-year inactive contract with the United States Marine Corps. You are a Marine, and you will have to follow the rules and regulations that govern us. You could easily be thrown into the brig and they would just hold you there until you comply."

"Put me in jail for wanting the correct MOS?" I shouted scornfully. "Is that a crime? Is that being insubordinate, wanting what I was promised?"

The Senior told me he would tell the other drill instructors I wasn't feeling well so I could take the day off to clear my head. I left his office and lay in my bunk for the remainder of the day. Shortly after, the rest of the platoon came back to the barracks. They all showered and went to bed. I kept thinking about the conversations I had with multiple officers and the Senior. I decided that I would try to convince them that I was mentally unstable in hopes that I would get kicked out of the Marine Corps. I thought about so many other failed attempts and the Marines that ended up in the brig instead of being sent home. I thought about all of the Marines that pretended to be gay in hopes of being kicked out and they, too, were unsuccessful. I prayed to God for strength and guidance.

Before I fell asleep, I decided to tell any high ranking official that I would hurt myself. I planned to cite depression was the cause of my suicidal ideations. The next morning, I pretended to be sick to separate from all of my peers, of whom admired or looked up to me. One of the drill instructors ordered me to report to medical. This drill instructor had questionable character because he always seemed to take extra care whenever punishing or yelling out obscenities to the black Marines. Unfortunately for me, while sick, I was allowed to take a shower alone, but the water for some reason was freezing cold. The gruesomely cold water stung my skin so I opted not to shower at all. When asked by that drill instructor, I told him I didn't shower because I was ill and the shower was extremely cold. That drill instructor told me the water was hot and to get back into the shower. I walked begrudgingly back to the shower, turned it on and stood away from it while pretending to shower. That was until the drill instructor walked into the shower area and ordered me to get underneath the shower head. He stood there with a keen sense of prominence and power as my lips quivered and body trembled in the cold water. This was gratifying for him in the highest degree. He stood there the entire time to ensure I didn't move away from the cold water. I later revealed this incident to the Senior drill instructor, who assured me that he would address the instructor's unacceptable behavior and he offered his most sincere apologies for what I experienced.

One of the very first acts in my life as it relates to inspiring someone occurred when I was being processed out of the USMC. I was accompanied with several other Marines who were standing on a bank overlooking the beautiful waters of the Pacific Ocean. The drill instructors escorting us pointed to a group of kids about fifty yards away. They were also admiring the ocean. The drill instructors told us that all of those children had cancer and had a life expectancy of three to four years. They encouraged us to go over and speak with the kids if we liked, but added that this wasn't mandatory of us. Most, if not all of us, stood there, motionless, and didn't attempt to make contact with the kids. I stood there confused because I assumed they were some lucky kids who were enjoying a nice vacation in sunny California. I waited a few seconds to follow the lead of the first guy who volunteered to speak to the kids until I realized no one did. So I became that guy. Soon after I departed, several others followed me. The kids were so amazed with us. We hardly got a chance to say anything to them since we were bombarded with question after question. "Mister...Mister...what's that?" One of the kids asked while pointing at one of my peers' fatigue trousers. "Are you a soldier? I never saw a real-life soldier before!" It was remarkable how appreciative those little kids were. But I was saddened when I thought about how often kids like them are cheated out of life and often overlooked. It seems that, somehow, man has become so occupied with helping himself that he's forgotten the compassion he once had when he was a child. Although I never saw those kids after that day, years later, I would fight in a charity boxing event to support kids just like them.

Sticking to my fake suicide plan, I went to medical and told the nurse that I wasn't feeling well. When asked, I told the nurse that I had a cold and that I was suffering from suicidal thoughts. That conversation was the start of a series of psychological evaluations and interviews by a team of psychologists and officials for several days. I was ultimately placed in a transitional barrack with many others who were being processed out of the USMC. In my new barracks, I met many people who were injured, mentally ill, and emotionally disturbed. Some were actors like me, and there were those who had legitimate reasons for being there. I had a final interview with an official who had the last say on whether or not I would be discharged. He said he didn't believe the things I had told everyone.

"You don't have any mental problems. You just don't want to be here." He called me a liar and said he was discharging me because I wasn't fit for the Marines. I walked back to my barracks happy and amazed.

Once the USMC released me, I had to get another psychological evaluation at a psychiatric hospital. Piece of cake, I thought, until I was told I was ordered to stay there for a minimum of three days. I wasn't allowed to leave because I was under military orders. Once admitted to the psych ward, the hospital assumed full authority over me. I met many people from the civilian world. I was the only soldier there. Because of this, many assumed I became mentally ill resulting from battle. That place was a far cry from the transitional barracks at Camp Pendleton because the people there were truly in dire need of mental treatment and psychiatric medication. Many of the patients talked to invisible beings and furniture. It was a telling moment for me and even somewhat humbling. I became well acquainted with one of the patients there, and he started teaching me to play chess. He took a strong interest in me and I shared the same sentiment for him. Upon my departure from the hospital, he wrote me a note and wished me well. I still have that note tucked carefully inside my high school yearbook. The note read, 'Be positive and keep a positive mind frame and positive things will come to you.' It also said to take the meds, don't let the meds take me. He was an amazing guy who many considered paranoid schizophrenic, but to me he was a friend. I had a debit card and the Corps deposited my final check on it the day I left the hospital. Military personnel arrived and escorted me to a bus station somewhere in Los Angeles. I guess they figured they spent too much money flying me out there so I should take the bus back. We hung out in downtown LA for a while and went to the mall. I marveled at the tall buildings and the city skyline. A few hours later, it was time to go and I was taxied to the Greyhound bus terminal.

I called Madea while I was still at the hospital to work out living arrangements. She said I could stay with her, but only on a temporary basis. I was unhappy about the situation regarding my MOS and became even more upset after being processed out of the United States Marine Corps. I was sad because I had done very well and I loved being a part of something. Plus, I planned on adopting my siblings while enlisted, but I wasn't thrilled about being forced into infantry for an unspecified time. I wanted to choose my career path as everyone else had, but my untruthful recruiter stole that opportunity away from me. I wasn't given a DD214 (discharge papers), but I received it by mail. My discharge status was classified as a medical discharge. I entertained the idea of one day reenlisting and selecting a MOS before basic training started.

Less than a few months after my discharge on September 20, 2001, President Bush declared "War on Terror" in the wake of the 911 attacks. This was a great moment of disparity as I wished I was still enlisted to exercise my right and privilege to defend my country. My mother would later comfort me by telling me that maybe it was God's will that I was never supposed to be in the Marines. The pain persisted and I felt guilty because I knew I should've been deployed into Iraq and Afghanistan with the thousands of brave souls who fought to secure the safety and sovereignty of this great and mighty nation. It was estimated that nearly three thousand Americans lost their lives during the senseless and tyrannical 911 attacks.

My uncle Andrew picked me up at the bus station near the airport once I arrived in Memphis. When I made it to Madea's house, I thanked her for accommodating me and walked across the street to my shack. Madea sent Andrew to tell me that I could sleep in her home with my younger sisters and brother if I wished. I thought for a second about what I was being told and wondered if I was hallucinating.

"Brad... Brad, do you hear me?"

"What?... Yeah, I heard you. Are you sure she said that, Andrew?"

Madea had her moments when she would be kind to me, but those moments didn't occur very often. I quickly learned to enjoy them while they lasted.

Academics

Coaches Curt Wittman and Terry Jackson contacted me about being a part of the Clark State University's (CSU) football program. I was also talking to a recruiter from an art school in Los Angeles. I was very interested in the art school and was fascinated with the idea of returning to California, Los Angeles in particular. I spoke with both schools for a couple of weeks. They argued strongly why I should attend their schools. I had to walk from Madea's house to the Fast Mart to use the pay phone to speak to the schools because she wouldn't allow me to use her phone. It was nice of her to allow me to stay with my siblings for the first time ever, but I was still met with her hatred. To her defense, her hatred had faded from completely extreme to a milder sort of hostility. She didn't abuse me physically anymore and her hate-filled rants weren't as hurtful as they once were. I kept coins in my pocket and often guarded the pay phone when I anticipated important calls. By this time the USMC sent me a small check for an unresolved balance they owed me. I cashed and spent it the same day. Realizing the check stub looked identical to the check, I took it to the convenience store and cashed it as well.

I visited my mother in jail and asked her for advice. She was more supportive of me attending school at CSU rather than going away to California again. A few days later, I decided to attend school at CSU instead of The Art Institute of California-Los Angeles.

I visited my mother before I departed for CSU. It was well over a three-hour drive from Glendale. CSU is located within the small township of Midland, Tennessee. I apologized to my mother for failing to complete the Marine Corps basic training. I promised that she would see me graduate from CSU since the warden wouldn't grant her the liberty to be escorted only a few blocks from the jail to attend my high school graduation. Mother smiled, hugged me, and told me she was proud and excited about me going to college. She referred to a high school librarian that suggested I wasn't smart enough to go to college. The librarian encouraged me to consider attending a trade school instead. Mother and I shared a lot of big moments while she was incarcerated, and my going off to college was one of those moments. At the time, I didn't see the grandness or the brevity of my plight. I only felt that, since I had realized who I was in Christ, I knew living a wild and crazy life wasn't for me anymore. "When I was a child I thought like a child and acted like a child, but when I became a man I put childish things away" -Apostle Paul

Apart from my short stint in the USMC, being in Midland was the first time I had control over my life and exercised the power to choose where I lived. Other than that, I would find shelter and refuge with whoever felt compassion for me and understood my hardships. I would sleep in crack houses or hang in the streets all night. I always refused to go to sleep whenever I stayed overnight on a street corner because my pride wouldn't allow me to do so. There may have been one isolated occasion or two when I did the contrary, but that seldom occurred.

At CSU, I didn't have to live with anyone or hang in the streets all night anymore. I enjoyed the luxury of having running water, lights, heat, and air conditioning. My first semester at CSU was chaotic. Standing in long lines all day, waiting to have my financial aid processed felt very much like being on the corner every day. Except this time it was for something positive. I wasn't violent nor was anyone violent towards me. I didn't have to look over my shoulder every five minutes for someone who wished to rob me, take my life or retaliate against me for something I had done. College life was good. It gave me a chance to be a kid. I had been on my own since I was seven and I had been living in the street since the age of twelve. On the other hand, not being oppressed or abused opened up the stage which highlighted many issues I didn't realize I had.

I realized these problems once I arrived in Midland. After arriving on campus, I was greeted by a few of my old high school varsity football teammates. Also, my good friend Brian and I were roommates. It was pretty cool having him as a roommate. Soon after I arrived in Midland, I met a young lady and fell instantly in love with the idea of being part of a family. She had a beautiful daughter, who was abandoned by her biological father.

My transition into CSU went well. I attended class as scheduled and started practice with the football team. After a few weeks, I moved in with my girlfriend and became the father her daughter never had. It was hard for me, being able to eat freely without being abused or ridiculed when I did. I recall once asking my girlfriend after she cooked a dinner to prepare a plate for me. I didn't ask because I desired to be waited on, but because I was uncomfortable and even a little afraid to go into the kitchen and get my own food. That was something I was never allowed to do. She politely prepared a handsome plate of food fit for a hardworking laborer. I looked at the plate with surprise. *All of this for me*, I pondered. I had a few odd moments like this one and it took time getting adjusted. This was quite an embarrassing moment for me during that time as I found myself hoarding food that I bought with my own money. I didn't realize I was doing this at first. It was a learned behavior since childhood. It was somewhat of a survival instinct. I used to sneak into the kitchen when my girlfriend was asleep or in class and feast. I just didn't feel comfortable with being comfortable. The Condescending Five made sure I felt that way.

Several months into our relationship, we conceived a child. Weeks prior to this, I was an unproven guy as it relates to sex. Some would even say that I was prudish. In describing my funniest and most shameful moment in reference to making love, it instantly puts a smile on my face and brings me to laughter. It happened when I was lying on the floor, watching television. My girlfriend walked into the living room wearing lingerie and stood over me. I looked up at her from the floor and wondered if I were in a real-life HBO *After Dark* love scene. This was my first time seeing a woman in lingerie. "Come here," I said as I grabbed a hold of her hand and guided her down onto the floor. She straddled me. Then she gently began to caress the lower extremity of her body, below her waist, against mine, until "it" was guided more or less perfectly inside her. Like a piece to a puzzle fitting into in unequal space, but not exactly flush. There was a portion of it protruding out. It was wet, it was warm. Deep moans of passion quickly ensued as she reeled her body backwards and forwards, alternating rhythms from slow to fast. Her body atop mine was interchanging between circular, horizontal, and vertical motions. Then, she worked her way right back into her original stride. After a time, sweat beaded down her back until it rested in the puddle that formed on my lower abdomen. As I saw in a late-night flick, I began slapping her across her butt firmly. Her sex cry and groans suggested she relished in it.

"Harder! Harder! Slap it, harder!" And I did. *Wham!* My eyes bucked and silence followed. I felt a throbbing unlike I ever had before as the numbing pain traversed my body. It caused me to ball into a knot and cry out.

"Shit! Baby are you okay?" She reached out her hand and attempted to comfort me.

"Don't touch me. My balls hurt! I'll be alright." I couldn't believe it. I had mistakenly struck myself in the testicles while I was smacking her on her ass. Although I didn't see her laugh, I'm certain she found the time to laugh at some point.

I was now faced with corresponding time between football practice, work, college, and being a family man. All of which I knew nothing about, but I had the love and compassion to try. I got a job at a local grocery store, Ultra Whole Foods. I was an overnight stocker and was very proud of my job. My girlfriend started pressuring me to quit the football team. Unknown at the time, it was because of her jealousy. She had complained once that other women might take interest in me because I had been lifting weights and working out too much. Not to mention the celebrity that was associated with being a part of the team. I disagreed and tried very hard to make things work.

I started showing up to the morning workouts late and exhausted from working overnight. I worked from 10:00 PM until 7:00 AM, and went directly to our strength and conditioning training after that. The strength coach liked me because he knew I was in the Marine Corps and he retired from the Navy. Whenever my teammates came to training late he would make them run a mile, but whenever I came in late he would greet me with a smile. He would often ask, "You're the guy from the Marines, right?" I'd nod my head and walk into the weight room, hoping he didn't make me run and he never did. I started missing my morning classes because I slept most of the day resting from the long shift I worked the previous night. I couldn't keep up with everything so I started alternating between missing practice and class but never missed work. I was proud to be taking care of my family and have someone to share my love with. I decided to quit the football team and that was a very hard decision. I missed nearly a month of practice and decided to have a talk with the coach.

Coach Jackson was happy to see me. "Hey Brandon, where you been? Boy, we missed you. I was worried about you. I thought you dropped out of school." I assured my coach that I wasn't going to drop out of school. However, I broke the news that I had decided to quit football. I told him that I had a pregnant girlfriend who also had a daughter to care for. Coach was very generous and offered to assist me with child care expenses so that I could continue playing football. This same coach had opened up his home to me when I first arrived in Midland to live there rent free. I thanked the coach, but insisted on working and taking care of my own responsibilities. He asked me to make sure I didn't drop out of school and I reassured him that I wouldn't quit. He extended his welcome for me to return to football at any point I decided to come back. After shaking his hand, I walked out of his office deeply saddened. On my way out, I ran into a couple buddies who also played football and I told them I had just quit the team.

I continued to work and started attending class more often. I also got a second job working at a temp agency on my off days. I was up at four in the morning, waiting in line with a large group of men who were mostly homeless and drug addicts. A guy with a clipboard would call the first five people and turn everyone else away. Sometimes, the temporary assignments lasted for only a day, and others nearly a month.

After several months, I resigned from Ultra Whole Foods and accepted a position in the mental health field as a residential counselor. I also worked part-time at Davis County Detention Center. My daughter confused my correctional officer uniform with that of a police officer.

My girlfriend and I visited the doctor's office and discovered we were having a baby boy. I was happy to learn of this. However, we began to have problems, primarily regarding her father. He was the kind of man who earned a decent living and felt as though that made him in some way superior to those less fortunate. My girlfriend kept her father involved in our relationship and allowed him to dictate our lives. One incident, concerning our bills, topped the list. One month, we didn't have enough money to pay both the light and telephone bill. I gave her what little money I had to pay the light bill before I left for work. The next morning, when I arrived home from work, I discovered that our apartment was completely dark. My girlfriend said she decided to pay the phone bill instead. She had done this so her father wouldn't know we didn't have money to pay the bill. She decided to pay the phone and have us live in our apartment without lights.

We separated many times before and during her pregnancy because of similar spats. Mostly, we fought about her and her father wanting an abortion. They both cited the economic hardship of having a second child. I asked my girlfriend how she would feel if she were the fetus being debated. Would she prefer to be killed by her parent and forfeit life? Wouldn't she choose life if she had the choice? She said something to the effect of, "Why wouldn't I choose to live?" I deplored her and her father's rebuttals and tactics.

Many weeks of this sort of debate continued between us. Her father sent relentless emails encouraging abortion in a subtle enough manner to leave room for denial if later challenged. I told my girlfriend that if she got an abortion, I would leave her. I wouldn't be able to bear the pain of losing my son. I loved her, her daughter, and our unborn son. I begged her not to get an abortion.

My son Jordan was born July 18, 2003, less than a year after our daughter died in a drowning accident. She drowned in her grandfather's swimming pool in Trenton, New Jersey.

Our daughter's funeral service was interrupted by her estranged biological father, and his brother and sister. They were Muslims. My daughter's aunt became upset because their names weren't listed on the program. She stood in front of the pulpit and started shouting in an unknown language as our pastor was delivering the eulogy. I was shocked, puzzled, and angered. I looked around for church security, hoping they would remove her. After she finished shouting only God knows what, she abruptly stormed back to her seat. Just as our pastor tried to make light of what just happened and offered his apologies, our daughter's uncle pranced up the aisle to the front of the congregation. He seemed to be trying to make amends for his sister's disruption, therefore, I restrained myself from wrapping my hands around his throat and tearing him to pieces. But once I realized this crafty fellow wasn't sincere in his statements as he began to hurl insults at my family, I leaped out of the pew like a gazelle unrestrained. My poor mother jumped up as quickly as she could to stop her "baby" from attacking this damned man.

I fought through the crowd that formed between me and my daughter's alienated uncle. My blazer buttons popped and I slipped out of it as I was struggling to pass my family. My cousin Daniel and friend Brian took hold of the silly bastard and removed him from the church. As they were doing this, my daughter's "sperm donor" attempted to make a scene, but he, too, was quickly overpowered and thrown out, as well. All of them were speedily escorted out of the sanctuary and my daughter's service resumed without further incident.

Once service was concluded, we arrived at the burial site. My daughter's estranged, crazed family showed up there, too. Luckily for them, no one caused any problems. One memorable moment I have of my daughter is when I saw her staring at a police officer at her school. A year later, that officer became a close friend of mine. I loved the way she admired the police and, as a result, I thought about becoming one. It was May 2004 when my baby girl passed away at the age of five and three months later her daddy became a police officer. I longed to see my daughter's face light up when she saw daddy in his new uniform. But this was a dream never to be realized. Her younger brother shared her enthusiasm regarding policeman. When he was about sixteen months he used to wear my "trooper hat". Whenever he saw a police car he would yell, "Daddy!" I had a beautiful family and I loved both my kids.

My girlfriend and I parted ways for good after countless failed attempts to keep her father out of our relationship. Without coming to terms with losing my daughter, I felt as though I had, in turn, lost my son, too. In a real sense, I did. I visited him regularly, but nothing compares to living in the same house. After our split, I began to focus my full attention on the police department and excelled.

Restitution

Becoming a police officer was one of my proudest and weirdest moments. I remember, as a little kid, playing cops and robbers. I always played the cop. Not because I wanted to, but because no one else wanted to. Since I was the youngest, I was stuck with it.

The culture of being a policeman is divided, as it is with most of America. The world of law enforcement is divided by racial, social, and economic status. I witnessed many incidents where white suspects, male or female, weren't arrested when there was probable cause. On the other hand, with cases involving black suspects, arrests would be made every time. In many cases arrest would be made without probable cause. I witnessed and was informed of police officers using excessive force when dealing with black suspects and complainants. When I looked to the department officials for corrective actions to be taken against this behavior, nothing was ever done. It became apparent that ill treatment of blacks and other minorities are acceptable practices in law enforcement, as well as in criminal and civil law.

I was a Police Officer in the city of Garland, which bordered Midland. On my first day out of the police academy, I was met with piercing and unwelcoming stares from many of my coworkers. I suppose they wondered why the Chief hired a nigger, and even worse, one that wasn't from Garland. The department at that time was overwhelmingly white, with about five minorities within the entire police force. Of those, two were detectives, and the other three worked in patrol, as I did. When I walked into shift change, the Lieutenant introduced me and I politely waved to everyone, only to receive blank stares. I was called a 'monkey' by a white police officer during my first week. He said it in roll call in front of everyone, but he said it low enough for me to cowardly pretend not to hear it. After a while, most of the department warmed up to me. As most rednecks in the Deep South would say, "He's not so bad for a black fella."

There was one officer I hit it off instantly with. Officer Dykes was a very brave and fair guy. He didn't seem to care that most of the department kept me at a distance. He made sure I felt welcomed. I had a difficult but humorous time adjusting to life as a cop. I was nervous my first time getting into the police cruiser with other officers. One time, when I was in the parking lot of the police department the dispatcher gave out a hot call (911 dispatched). Seconds later, officers ran outside and yelled for me to get in as they hopped into their cruisers. I bolted over to the closest cruiser and squeezed myself into the caged back seat and slammed the door shut. I hit the glass of the prisoners' cage to signal to the other officer that I was ready to go. The officer had a puzzled look on his face.

"Get the hell out of the back seat! Get in the front. What the hell is wrong with you?" The officer was dying laughing.

That was a hilarious moment and it took a while to live it down.

There was another time recently after I was hired. I, along with several other officers, responded to a disturbance involving a large crowd of drunken club goers. I was one of the first to arrive on the scene and immediately radioed for backup. When the cavalry came, they came in full force. I saw the flashing red and blue lights at a distance and heard the sirens as they wailed. The officers bailed out of their cruisers without delay and ran towards the crowd. They dispersed as quickly as they had assembled. The funny thing was that I, too, was startled. I took a few steps back and thought about running with the crowd. For a black man, especially in the South, the sight of six white men running at you with AR-15 assault rifles can prove frightening, even as a police officer.

Officer Dykes (Tristen) was my field training officer. He and I became good friends, establishing an unbreakable bond. He was fair and impartial, unlike many of the other officers within the department. This earned him a great deal of respect from me and the entire black community. It was awesome having Tristen as my FTO. We shared plenty of fun moments unsparingly.

by Brandon Williams

One time, Tristen and I responded to a hot call in a high crime area. While en route to the call, he told me to handle whatever we are faced with. He would be there only to assist me, as my current phase of training suggested. It was time to prove I could function independently of my FTO. When we arrived in the housing projects, I saw a dirty man with dingy, grey dreadlocks that looked more like...well, shit-locks. He was arguing with someone and Tristen stepped in to quell the situation and apologized for doing so.

Looking at me, Tristen said, "This is your show. Take control of the situation."

I approached the mild-mannered gentleman and asked him what was going on. He turned around hasty and began to tear me a new ass whole. I couldn't think of anything to say, so I kept shouting repeatedly, "Sir! Sir! Sir, I need you to calm down!"

The suspect's response was something to the effect of, "Shut the hell up you fucking pig! Get off my block."

I knew the suspect was rumored to have AIDs and I wasn't willing to put my hands on him if it were avoidable. Soon after, other officers arrived on the scene. I'm sure every officer assisting us wondered how long I was going to stand there, allowing this guy to rant. I manned up and yelled out a few verbal commands, but the suspect never relented. Tristen and the other officers took over the scene and we were 10-8 (back in service) from that location. When asked why I didn't arrest the guy for disturbing the peace while using profanity, I simply said, "I didn't know I could."

Near the end of my field training I had redeemed myself, to say the least, minus one other rookie cop blooper. It was my very last day of field training and Tristen told me that, depending on how I preformed, he would recommend that I be certified. Certification meant that I could function as an officer independent of an FTO. I went through most of the shift with ease. I responded to and handled several hot calls, including domestic violence, drug related calls, and a couple of car crashes. I made several arrests and completed all of my reports in a timely manner. Tristen was smiling; he always held that I turned out to be a good officer. It was towards the end of the shift when we drove into the Waffle House parking lot. We got a bite to eat and chatted for a while. Shortly after, we got back into our cruiser and I started driving towards the police department. It was around five in the morning. I unknowingly made a left turn onto a two-lane, one-way street when Tristen gave me a very startled gaze. I assumed it was because I said something that he didn't agree with. But then I wondered if I might have said something extremely profound and I shocked poor Tristen by speaking with immeasurable wisdom.

I continued to drive down the street and Tristen started whistling and turned his face away from me. He put his hand on his head and out of nowhere a car comes barreling in my direction, head on. I swerved into another lane to void the crash. Just as I was screaming "Oh shit!" at the top of my lungs, two more cars darted by. I looked at Tristen and said, "I can't stop all of the cars for traveling the wrong way, but I will get at least one of them." I proceeded to turn around to give chase.

"Brandon, do you really think all of those cars are going the wrong direction?"

At that point, I realized I was the car that needed to be stopped by an officer. I had been traveling the wrong way while telling Tristen, the whole time, how ready I was to be on my own. He was too flabbergasted with my reaction when I saw the oncoming traffic to be upset with me. I believe he may have felt that his endless laughter and my humiliation was discipline enough.

Those were my virgin days as an officer. I didn't know if I would truly enjoy being an officer or not, but I was more focused on proving myself and so I did. I became popular in the community with the young and old. I gained the support and trust of the majority of the people in Garland and Midland. I was well known and loved.

I had an unforgettable experience when I was working a single car crash. I nearly caused a second crash involving about three or four women. They were passing by the scene of the car crash and started waving. I didn't recognize the women, so I thought they were waving to the man who wrecked his car. I turned to him and smiled, saying, "Looks like you have a car full of admirers, Sir."

He smiled back. "I wish, but I don't know those women." He pointed in their direction and said, "Look!"

I turned back, what I saw could've very well been taken out of a Hollywood movie script. The women had been admiring me, and mistakenly turned down a one-way street. Instead of driving straight ahead, as they had been, they turned quickly onto the one-way street to continue looking at me, not paying attention.

I yelled, "Hey! What are you doing? That's a one-way street!"

They smiled, waved, made some comments I need not mention and continued driving. The sound of car horns and angry drivers yelling obscenities soon got their attention. They quickly swerved into a convenience store parking lot, safely out of harm's way. Once I finished working the crash, the gentleman thanked me and humorously remarked, "You almost had a second crash to work." I laughed and told him I had no idea what I would've cited as the cause of their crash for their insurance company. I could've written a citation for being too flirtatious while driving, if there were such a charge.

Another time, the dispatcher gave me a call regarding a suspicious person near an apartment on the east side of town. That area had its fair share of crime. I responded to the apartment. It was located in the housing projects. I clutched my weapon and searched the immediate vicinity for anyone or anything that appeared to be out of place. It was around 3:00 AM on a weekday and the area was quiet. No one was on the street besides me, other officers, and presumptively some unfaithful spouse's that were nothing more than whispers in the wind. I was baffled that there was no one on the block after receiving a suspicious person call. I left the apartment complex, parking on a nearby street, and turned off the engine. I got out of my cruiser to listen for any noise or movement. Minutes later, I keyed up on my radio and reported the matter unfounded to the dispatcher and left the scene (10-8).

I circled the apartment complex again and left the area. Less than two minutes later, the dispatcher radioed me again regarding the same call for service. I was advised that the complainant requested to speak with me. I returned to the apartment complex, walked up to the apartment unit, and knocked on the door. No one answered, but it was left partially open. This is a common practice, leaving the door open for law enforcement officers to walk in, and in most cases, we do. After a couple more knocks, I heard a woman's voice say, "Come in, come in, it's open."

I entered the residence after speaking to dispatch one more time for confirmation, and it was completely dark.

An officer requested over the radio, "Cruiser 1865, let me know if you need backup so we can start coming your way."

"Copy that, I'll let you know in a second."

There was a dim light illuminating from the bedroom and the woman asked me to enter, so I did. I was met with the tan, glistening skin of a lovely lady. The sheets wrestled to cover the many curvatures of her flawless body. She was lying in her bed completely undressed, as if she were a military wife waiting to surprise her husband.

Oh my God! Had I heard this woman correctly? Did I mistakenly walk into her bedroom while she was unclothed? I was startled and yelled out, "Sorry, Ma'am!" and turned to exit her bedroom.

"Don't go! Your fine. I called you in here to talk to you" she said casually.

"What! What, are you saying? I'm sorry, but I can't stand here while you lie in bed naked." As I was walking out to the living room, I asked how she knew I would be the responding officer.

"I know when you work this area." She smiled shyly.

Apologizing, I told her I had to leave. I suggested she get dressed and lock the door after I left. Although I said this, I wanted to say something totally different, and she hoped I would. It was apparent that she called me to her apartment that night to indulge in an erotic evening with Officer Friendly.

This young lady and I attended Clark State University (CSU) together. I saw her on campus many times and we greeted each other with an occasional "hello" or "how's it going", but that was as far as it went. I saw her once before this when I worked at Davis County Correctional Center. She visited an inmate there. I didn't even know her name. Only a brief "hi" and "bye" in passing was the gist of our interaction. Although I must say, like most guys at CSU, I thought she was remarkably attractive. I never dreamed she would've taken the approach she chose that night. I told her I had to leave and I would see her on campus. I walked out of her apartment with mixed emotions, accompanied with a million thoughts. I was as confused as a, well, I can't seem to think of a comparison; one that would rightfully detail my mental anguish. Why hadn't I stayed? What was I thinking? God help me. My flesh was weak.

I closed her front door and walked to my car. Sliding into my cruiser, I advised the dispatcher I was 10-8. I drove away recounting the whole incident in utter amazement, drunken off lust.

Only in a movie would something like that happen. I told a couple officers while winding down from a long day. I was scarfing down an egg, ham, and cheese omelet. This was one of my favorites whenever I ate at the Waffle House. I saw that young woman many times afterwards and neither of us ever spoke about what happened. I suffered great distress imagining how things could have turned out if I hadn't walked out of her bedroom that night. She knew I had mixed feelings about the whole thing because she would smile at me in just the right way to let me know that she knew.

But when I responded to my first domestic violence call, it was a totally different experience.

I reverted to that seven-year-old kid who used to witness his mother being beaten by her lover. Several officers arrived on the scene at the same time.

Knock, knock, knock.

"Police open up. Garland Police open up!"

No one answered. We banged on the door harder, hearing the commotion of the attack. I could hear the sound of a firmly clinched fist colliding into someone's body. A sound I was all too familiar with. And then a woman screamed.

The apartment walls vibrated from the force of the victim's body crashing against it. Finally, the order was given for us to force entry into the home. One officer shoved his shoulder into the door, but he was humiliatingly unsuccessful. I motioned for the officer to step aside and I kicked the door in. It swung open forcefully, striking a wall, and bounced back. I rested my hand against it as we rushed in with guns drawn, ordering the man to the ground. He refused.

"Down, down, down on the ground! Now!"

I, along with another officer, grabbed him and threw him against the wall, placing him under arrest.

I escorted him out of the home to place him in my cruiser. The other officers stayed back to interview the victim. I'm not sure how, but while I was walking the suspect to my cruiser, the victim came from nowhere and started beating him in the back of his head with her fist. I stepped in front of her, attempting to stop her from attacking a defenseless man. Then something came over me. I was arrested by the pain and long suffering of the millions of battered women. I was paralyzed and gripped with sorrow, somehow unable to move. My legs became numb and that woman walked around me and handed down the worst ass whipping I had ever witnessed. I clinched my bottom lip with my teeth as I looked on. Damn that had to hurt. She punched and scratched her abuser senseless. I can only imagine the next morning; he probably looked like he had walked into a lion's den, but not as lucky as Daniel.

I questioned myself at times and wondered if I really was unable to stop the attack. Or did I simply allow this woman to whip her abuser's ass? At any rate, he had it coming, if not from her, from someone who cared about her.

"Brandon, what the hell are you doing? Stop her!" one of my coworkers yelled. A couple officers seized her and led her back inside her apartment. I could've lost my job for that, but for some reason I just didn't care.

I had many interesting experiences as a police officer. Another one that comes to mind is when I rescued several people from an apartment fire. It happened early in the morning hours, following a long day of responding to 911 calls hour after hour. The dispatcher broadcasted an apartment building engulfed in flames. The dispatcher mentioned there were loads of residents reportedly inside. Within minutes, the building was flooded with police lights and yelping sirens. Several police officers responded promptly. We arrived on scene surprisingly before EMT medics and fire engines. Lacking prior experience and training, we ran up the stairs to assist residents with no thought of the danger we were placing ourselves in. Midway up, we realized it was a good idea to remove our duty belts. Our duty belts contained a service weapon (i.e. gun), pepper spray, and ammunition, which were combustible. We removed our belts, designated an officer to secure them and ran back to the burning building.

I bolted upstairs to the second floor with a couple of the officers while the others probed the bottom level for occupants. We operated as a skeleton search and rescue team.

"Police, Police, you have to evacuate safely and orderly! This building is on fire."

by Brandon Williams

We kicked in a few doors to confirm those units were vacant after knocking and receiving no answer. The ironic thing was that the fire occurred on a Sunday morning around 2:00 AM. Most of the residents were college students, and many were avid partygoers. Luckily enough, over half the building was vacant with the exception of those who were in bed, already hung-over. I banged on one guy's door. He opened it, asking, "Is there a problem, Officer? I didn't do anything wrong."

There was fire and smoke blazing from every direction.

"Get out! Get out now before I carry you out." I continued on to the next apartment. The guy quickly exited the apartment and hurled himself safely down the stairwell. There were a couple other humorous incidents but that drunken kid tops the chart. How could he not have seen the flames and smoke roaring behind me? Or did he think I was a fire breathing dragon who just so happened to be a police officer?

We had most of the building evacuated before the fire department arrived. That was a very fulfilling day. A resident, who was also a student, recognized me from CSU and a veteran officer offered, "Job well done." We all got back into our cruisers and an officer radioed to the dispatcher, "No reported injuries and the fire has been extinguished, 10-8."

Racism and Law Enforcement

A few months later, I participated in an annual boxing event held in Houston, Texas. In the charity boxing event, policemen and firemen from all over the South participated. It was police versus firemen, and boy were those firemen big. A portion of the proceeds were donated to the United Way for Children and other charities, including a nonprofit organization that served kids living with chronic illnesses and disabilities. I never knew those kids would influence me so greatly. I intended on impacting their lives with encouraging words, but their resilience inspired me. They helped me rediscover an old passion I had nearly forgotten I had.

It was my genuine desire to help each and every individual in need within my reach. There are many ways to offer support but it is utterly meaningless if we never stop to ask someone in need, "How can I help you?" The faces of those little boys and girls I spoke with many years ago at camp Pendleton I can vaguely remember, but their little voices and stories I will remember forever.

I fought two years in the boxing event and won every bout, but the truth is, every participant was a winner. They were winners to those in need that rallied behind them, cheering for the police officer or fireman they favored to win. But it was an entirely different scene when a fight broke out while on duty.

I remember seeing police fight suspects prior to becoming a cop and criticized them for it. It wasn't until I became a cop that I understood why. If there were three policemen on a scene with one suspect and one of the officers got into a scuffle with the assailant, it would be expected that the other two officers would assist that officer. I can personally testify, in almost all cases, when you see a group of officers beating the life out of a minority, it is most likely racially charged. From my experience with many incidents such as these, officers will beat a minority, curse, and threaten them simply because they can. Minorities generally don't report cases of police brutality and misconduct. And most officers know this. I've witnessed whites and middle-class citizens file bogus police complaints many times over. But what keeps minorities silent eludes me.

There was an incident when one of our K9 officers attempted to apprehend a suspect on foot and I responded to assist him. While en route, I studied the transmissions the K9 officer made regarding their direction of travel. I parked a few blocks north and waited for the suspect. Once the suspect saw my cruiser, he walked in a different direction. I yelled out to him, "If you make me chase you, you're going to jail. But if you talk to me, you might have a slim chance of going free." The suspect was startled by my unexpected statement and walked towards my cruiser, placing his hands on the hood. I radioed to the dispatcher that I had the suspect in custody. I conducted a pat down for weapons or anything on or about his person that could be used as one. I placed the suspect in handcuffs and awaited the arrival of the K9 officer who was originally pursuing the suspect. While the suspect was handcuffed and leaning against the hood of my cruiser, the K9 officer grabbed his neck and slammed him into my car repeatedly. My initial reaction was to strike the officer in his face to defend this helpless man. After restraining myself from doing so, I stepped between the two of them in an attempt to keep the officer from attacking him further.

More officers, including a sergeant, later arrived on the scene and, witnessing this incident, intervened. I felt partly to blame because the suspect, as most of the blacks and other minorities in the community, believed that a large portion of the officers I worked with were racist. I imagine incidents such as this was the principal reason why the suspect refused to stop for the K9 officer. He was fearful he would become a victim of police brutality motivated by racism, and he was right. I believe that once he saw me, a black police officer, one with backbone, meaning I wasn't an 'uncle tom', he felt I wouldn't let anything bad happen to him. For days, I was upset not at the K9 officer but with myself. I felt as though I had failed the citizens I had sworn to protect. I swore and took an oath, but never imagined I would have to protect anyone from a police officer.

Despite the officer assaulting the suspect, he never filed an official complaint. I encouraged him to file a complaint and provided him with all the necessary information needed. I also gave him the badge number of the officer who attacked him. I told him whenever he spoke to an official regarding this incident to cite me as a witness. I would've corroborated his story. The guy was discontent with filing a formal complaint. He said "they all in it together. The officials are racist, too" in a loud, scornful voice. I must say, the points he made were factual and bore truth. If questioned, do I believe there are high ranking officials who wrongfully dismiss complaints of racial profiling and police brutality because they themselves are racist? Yes. I would also agree if asked if I believe this occurs every day in various industries and police departments. This has always happened and always will, until God changes it. It is my belief that people should stand up for themselves more. The guy who got attacked did not make a complaint, nor did he seek civil or criminal charges against the K9 officer. Instead, he felt compelled to complain to people in the community. That is not good enough. Behavior such as this invites more racist officers to brutally attack black and other minority suspects. These officers know no one will ever report them. Snitching isn't acceptable in urban America, although it should be. If the Blacks, Mexicans, or other ethnic groups took a stand, got out the video recording phones, and marched up to the local news or radio station with the evidence, the police departments would be forced to rethink their behavior. Racist officers have to kill a minority before anyone decides to speak out. But then it's too late. The deceased is lying in a pool of blood, overshadowed by false evidence. The invaluable facts that would bring them justice, discarded. There were many incidents similar to this that I witnessed or heard rumors about. Even minority police officers, including myself, have become victims to racially charged incidents. Some black police officers are worse than their racist white counterparts when dealing with the black community. These officers sometime feel the need to impress and fit in by racially profiling and unlawfully targeting black people. This kind of officer can be more dangerous than a racist white officer because he yearns to fit in, desperately.

Oxford Dictionary defines racism as prejudice, discrimination, or antagonism directed against someone of a different race based on the belief that one's own race is superior. I've also discovered there are different levels of racism. I will classify them based on the degree of social, physical, and financial harm each level has the propensity to cause. Racism First Degree (R-1) is the highest level. Those that possess this level of racism have the tendency to cause extreme extents of damage. R-1 are those who destroys property, brutally assaults, murders, or relish when this happens to someone. R-1 operates in many key positions today and this allows them to quietly exercise their prejudices, virtually unnoticed. Some examples of these positions are Police Officer, Correctional Officer, Judge, and Politician. Slave Owners, Slave Traders, Lynch Mobs and lynch mob spectators' best describes R-1's role during those days. Racism Second Degree (R-2) is the second highest level. The only difference between R-2 and R-1 is those who subscribe to this level do not desire to partake in the actions of R-1, but relishes when someone else does. An example of this is someone who revel when someone's property is destroyed, brutally assaulted, or murdered because of their race. Racism Third Degree (R-3) is the third level. Those that embrace this level are nonviolent. Although R-3 doesn't support violence they are the most problematic. They support and create laws, regulations, and practices which causes disadvantages for other races. Ideal professions for someone classified as R-3 are local, state, and federal government lawmakers. Today's unjust laws and practices are the foundation of R-3's work. Discriminatory laws of the past otherwise known as "Black Codes and Jim Crow" were drafted by people from this level. Racism Forth Degree (R-4) is the lowest form of racism. The people within this level do not promote violence or discriminatory laws. In fact this group advocates against ill treatment of other races. But this group maintains their race is superior to all others. Some of the abolitionist who fought to end slavery can easily be classified within this group.

Allow me to share with you a place where men and women openly discriminate and yell racial slurs. The only discipline they receive in regards to their behavior is to be asked why they are being so nice to those niggers, wet backs, spics, and every other derogatory term used to emasculate innocent minorities.

I recall a situation when two officers and I conducted a search of an abandoned house. The dispatcher said there was a report of an unlawful entry. While conducting the search, each of us was responsible for clearing a portion of the house. The term "clear" means there is no apparent threat of danger and no suspects are present within that specified area. In order for an officer to clear any area, he or she must visually scan the area with their weapons on target. Once this is done, the officer yells "clear!" so approaching officers will not search that same location again. This renders them totally vulnerable if an officer has not successfully cleared an area. Officers place their trust and livelihood into the hands of the officer that cleared the specified area. This is the nature of police work. Every officer, in some way, depends on another.

Another officer accompanied me and the officer I was partnered with. We arrived on scene of the abandoned house. The perimeter was checked for fleeing suspects. There were none. We entered the house. Once inside, we conducted a search for any person or persons. Officers yelled out "clear!" checking off that vicinity as safe. After searching the house and being exposed to areas the other officers said were clear, our search was complete. On the way out, my partner said the most startling thing.

"Hey guys, I didn't really clear that room right there. I just said I cleared it."

"Say what! You didn't do what? What if someone came out of that room right now with guns blazing?" I shouted.

"Awe, come on Brandon, do you want me to clear the room now for you?"

The three of us quickly scanned the room. Nothing was found. The three of us stormed out of the house immediately.

I radioed the dispatcher. "10-8 back in service."

I couldn't believe my partner had lied. Why would he say he cleared the room when he didn't? Why would he carelessly put the other officer's life and mine in danger? In many other incidents, police officers conducting searches have gotten ambushed. There were several cops killed in the line of duty that year in Tennessee by conducting searches and attempting to serve arrest warrants.

My partner's excuse for not searching the room was that an object was behind the door and he didn't want to force it open. I could have been killed over another cop's stupidity and the false information he had given. I was angry with him. We didn't talk for the remainder of our shift. I told a couple of officers what had happened and they could not believe it. In fact, some of them said my partner needed to be fired, while others thought a suspension would be sufficient. After a few days, I decided to bury the hatchet and move forward. I approached my partner and told him "No harm, no foul" but I was still curious as to why he lied. I wanted to know his mindset. His reply was shocking, he didn't think he had put my life at risk. Nor did he think the possibility of someone being injured by his actions were likely. He was both tactically and morally wrong. He displayed reckless disregard for human life, and that was unacceptable. He dismissed my concerns and quickly dispelled the idea that his actions were wrong in anyway. It appeared my attempts to squash the situation had only caused tensions to flare.

I was encouraged by other officers to inform an official about the situation. I responded similarly to the suspect who was assaulted by the K9 officer. "Those officials are suspect, racist." My thinking was also the mindset of most of the black people. My department was predominantly white, and many of them were long held as racist throughout black and white communities. Some of them were patrol officers, while some worked in specialized units or held ranking positions within the department. To make matters worse, the sergeant and lieutenant of my shift were very good friends with my partner. For the same reasons as the suspect the K9 officer had attacked, I decided not to report the matter. I only vented and went on occasional rants whenever I thought about it.

A day later I mentioned my concerns to a very close friend of mine. He was the FTO that trained me years prior. I told Tristen about what happened. I didn't give notice to his rank until he told me he had to report what happened because of it. He was a sergeant. He said my partner had been involved in a couple of other unfavorable incidents, to which he never got reprimanded for. I didn't want to report the incident because I feared officers who favored my partner would retaliate. If I made a complaint against a white officer, other white officers would strike back. Tristen agreed and said my partner would receive remedial training or suspension because of his negligence. I told him that I would report the matter myself.

By the end of my shift I had typed a short statement detailing the incident. I turned it in to the most senior lieutenant the following morning. He hurriedly scanned through the letter with a look of surprise and frustration. The lieutenant assured me he would take care of the matter. He said, "We have been watching him. You know how it is; he just doesn't know better." The lieutenant stood up, shook my hand, patted me softly on my back and walked me to the door.

"I appreciate your help, Lieutenant."

"Anytime, Brandon. If you have any more problems out of him, come see me."

He might as well have greeted me with the kiss of Judas Iscariot, the disciple who betrayed the Lord and savior Jesus. He kissed Jesus to signal to the roman soldiers that he was the one they should arrest to later crucify. It was around 10:30 or 11:30 AM when I turned in my statement. By that time the next day my partner, our shift corporal, sergeant, and lieutenant had statements against me drafted and laying on the senior lieutenant's desk.

The four of them launched a campaign against me. They started spreading false rumors in attempts to defame my character. For the most part, I give them credit because it worked. In fact, I imagine even today, years later, there are police personnel, officers, and officials that still hold distain for me because of these rumors. I'm not clear on what many of the rumors were about because no one ever told me. I got wind that one of them was that I thought I was too good for the department. This came about when I spoke to my shift sergeant about my hopes of one day becoming a pastor. One of the ways they built their case against me was when the corporal questioned me regarding a traffic crash we worked together. The corporal started sneering and yelling at me about the traffic crash. He did this in a manner similar to a furious father shouting at his unruly teenager. My partner was the only other person in the office when the corporal lost his temper. I wasn't surprised they planned this attack, but I was caught off guard by their tactics. The corporal stood over me while I was seated, and he continued shouting at me. My partner was seated a few feet to my right with his back turned to me. Although I couldn't hear him laughing, his faint, but constant chuckling caused his entire body to shake as the corporal demoralized me. The corporal's face was red and I wasn't certain if he planned to attack me physically. I sat there quietly as he scolded me. After he was done ranting, he pulled up his duty belt in satisfaction and sat down next to me. He began talking in a normal manner, as if nothing just occurred.

Once he settled himself, I looked at him and said with composure, "The next time you talk to me, please be mindful of your tone of voice and choice of words." I encouraged him to be as professional as possible. I suppose asking him not to shout and attempt to deflate my spirits caused him to become more irate. He jumped out of his seat and gazed at me. I, at once, stood up to prevent him from striking me while I was still seated. He grabbed his radio and yelled with great distress for his racist shift lieutenant and good friend. Almost instantly, in charges the lieutenant with a look on his face that screamed, *damn this feels good, you black bastard. We finally got something on you!*

"In my office now!" the lieutenant exclaimed without even knowing what occurred. Our shift sergeant also popped up out of nowhere and joined us in the lieutenant's office.

"What's the problem?" he asked.

"Sir, I'm fine. I don't have a problem," I responded.

"Oh what the hell, you were being a fucking smart ass and insubordinate and shit," the corporal bursts.

"I asked him to refrain from addressing me in that manner because I found it to be unprofessional and deliberately confrontational."

I was asked a slew of inequitable questions for several minutes. The lieutenant asked the corporal and sergeant to leave his office. He and I continued talking. He asked me personal questions, one being if I planned on retiring from the Garland Police Department. If it's the Lords will, I replied. I shared with him my long-held hopes to one day become a full-time pastor and public speaker. This statement, among others, he twisted, omitted, and added to, using them against me. Before the sergeant had left, he said, just like the lieutenant, "I'm fair and nobody is taking sides hear. But I'm telling you to your face, you were wrong for speaking to the corporal the way that you did."

"I'm wrong for questioning his blatant lack of common courtesy and respect?"

"Shut up! Shut up! That's enough! Now, I've had enough of your smart mouth," the lieutenant commented.

At that point I declined to speak or try to shield myself. It was reasonably clear, they were paying me back for reporting my partner, their good friend. The sergeant wasn't even present when the incident between the corporal and I took place. The trio was retaliating. They were bent on getting even and so they did.

They conferred amongst themselves and gave matching accounts of everything that took place, from alleged insubordination, having a smart mouth, and making a mistake on a crash report. This was done in desperate efforts to slander my name. I was perplexed when I heard the rumor that the sergeant who wasn't even present during the incident had written a statement against me.

I find it astonishing how far hatred of one's color, creed, or race can drive someone.

The corporal told me I didn't list all of the damage to one of the vehicles involved in the three-car crash. Once he finally calmed down, I corrected the mistake.

When I wrote my statement regarding my partner for not clearing a room and lying about it, my statement was made available to anyone who wished to see it, thus giving my partner an opportunity to know what he was being accused of. Then he could give his own account of what happened. I wasn't allowed to read the statements they wrote, nor was the information contained within them ever disclosed to me. Whenever I spoke with various officials regarding their statements, they brushed me off. I was being persecuted and I wasn't clear on what or why.

Even to this day, I have no knowledge of what those officers wrote in their statements. I concluded that reporting a white officer was not tolerated, no matter the circumstances. It will end in retaliation and false allegations. That's the primary message I gathered from the meetings with multiple officials. Many white officers who I thought were friends distanced themselves from me during that time, serving only to increase the racial gap already placed between the white and black officers.

One of our dispatchers asked the other, "Can you believe what they're saying about Brandon? He's just not that kind of person."

The other said, "Brandon's not like that, girl. He just made the wrong people mad, that's all it is."

As one officer who worked the same shift as I did put it, "Dammit Brandon, you know none of this would be going on if you wasn't black. I feel sorry for you, brother."

I asked with sarcasm, "Do you reckon it's my entire fault for being a black male?"

He sharply replied with a huge grin on his face, "Brandon, you're right. It's your fault. You had absolutely no business being black." The officer I was joking with was white, and he is an undeniably unbiased, All-American guy.

I laughed and so did he. I needed that humor because those days proved to be more stressful than all the years I was employed there. I grew weary and insecure of any officer that suddenly acted standoffish towards me. The word quickly spread that I was about to be fired or suspended for an unspecified amount of time. Many officers, white and black, encouraged me to hire an attorney. But I wanted to see how everything played out further before I sought the counsel of an attorney.

The senior lieutenant and other officials decided to make me and the corporal who ostracized me partners. As if the four of them hadn't done enough in retaliation. From being humiliated by the corporal, to the rumors of me being suspended or fired, and now they made us partners.

The corporal and I received a disturbance call involving multiple suspects. To the best of my memory, a large group of black females from Jamaica Queens, New York and some locals were assembled in front of a residence, partially in the roadway, shouting at each other, getting ready to fight. The dispatcher reported that the incident stemmed from a child custody dispute.

The corporal and I responded to the scene and observed about six to eight black women and two men screaming obscenities back and forth. They were yelling threatening words to each other. Once I parked the cruiser I exited the car with one thought in mind, and that was to protect the lives and welfare of those citizens. Chiefly, the small child one of the women had clutched in her arms. While I was getting out of the car, the corporal asked if I was "hot", which translates to if my body microphone was turned on.

"Yeah, I'm hot."

He stayed in the car. I assumed he would be getting out within a few seconds, given the nature of the call. As I approached the crowd it became rather apparent that the corporal had abandoned me. He refused to get out of the cruiser and assist with the riotous, chaotic crowd. Everyone was yelling and shouting at one another. I couldn't pinpoint the complainant because all of them appeared to be the aggressor.

The crowd moved from the roadway after ordering them several times to move onto the sidewalk next to my cruiser. I managed briefly to separate the two groups by sending one side into the house and keeping the other on the sidewalk with me. Seconds later, they came right back outside and stood in the yard, within ear shot of the other party and me. The yelling and screaming persisted. It began to attract the attention of bystanders, who congregated on nearby corners. A fight nearly ensued when the godmother walked out of her yard in a hurried fashion to confront the mother of the child they were feuding over. In response, the mother and those in support of her began walking in the godmother's direction.

"Stop! Hey! Stop," I commanded. "Shit," I mumbled scornfully under my breath. I was frustrated because the corporal sat in the safety of our cruiser and refused to assist after I had asked repeatedly.

A couple of bystanders that seemed to have taken a liking to me shouted, "Officer, you need some backup. They need to send more officers here." Then I pointed to the corporal and said, "There, that's my backup right there."

With a staggered look on her face, the bystander looked at the corporal, shook her head, and helped me diffuse the mob. I stood between both crowds, once again, and extended my arms to separate them. I was initially met with the same resistance as I received the first time I had separated them. But they soon complied. The mother walked away from the crowd and the godmother walked back into her yard. I told the two women to trust me and allow me to do my job. I promised to help them resolve their differences. I told them if anyone assaulted or made threats to a person, they would be arrested. Although, I knew I couldn't arrest anyone if the crowd didn't allow me to, since I was vastly outnumbered.

By this time, the crowd had grown upwards of twenty to twenty-five, not counting the blood-thirsty bystanders. I learned this lesson a couple of years earlier while trying to arrest someone who ran into a horde of several hundred people in a housing project. When I caught up to the suspect and was about to place him under arrest, the mass snatched him away from me. The suspect sunk deeper and deeper into the multitude until he was out of sight.

The mother complained by saying that she wanted her child's belongings out of the godmother's house. The godmother didn't want her to remove the belongings because she believed the mother would bring the child back once she calmed down. The backdrop to this story is that the godmother was the primary caregiver of the child. The mother, on the other hand, rarely found time between clubbing, wooing men, and abusing drugs to spend with her child. But that day was one of those rare moments. I saw the logic in both view points and I expressed that to them. I wrestled with alternative solutions to quell the situation. When I was doing so, the godmother and a couple of the bystanders asked where I was from because I didn't act like most of the officers they were accustomed to.

"I'm from the small-town of Glendale, Tennessee. It's located about three hours south of here. Have you heard of it before?"

"No, I don't believe I have."

I laughed and added, "Many people haven't heard of Glendale."

One of them said, "I like him. He's a cool cop."

I blushed and thanked them for the kind words. Somehow, I became the focus of both parties. I paced from the godmother's yard to the sidewalk, interviewing the mother to find a common ground. The godmother said I seemed to care about the people in the community and she thanked me for it. The women agreed to leave most of the child's things with the godmother and only take essential items.

This was one of my hardest calls for service ever. I was left stranded by the corporal to deal with a large crowd, of who were progressively growing angrier. I stole their hearts with the following reply to a series of questions they asked: "I try to be fair to everyone without respects to persons, gender, race, education, or economic status." I told them how I grew up in the street and lived a hard life early on.

The godmother and mother were very interested in my story and invited me to church. I was deeply flattered and told them I would be glad to visit their church. The godmother said I should give my testimony when I attended.

Nearly an hour had passed. The godmother and mother were walking away, and the crowd was dispersing. The corporal's face was red with grief.

I believed he and some officials had hoped for a moment like this, where I would get hurt or allow someone to get hurt. That way, they could cite me as being an incompetent officer, much like the officer I complained on. Some of the bystanders were pointing towards our cruiser, saying "Look at that white officer. He was in his car the whole time."

I re-entered the cruiser with a defiant sense of pride. The corporal didn't speak a single word to me all the way to the office. I couldn't imagine two riotous crowds enraged with unquenchable anger being controlled by one officer of any level. Typically, a call like that would require, at a minimum, seven or eight officers, if not more.

I reported the incident to the patrol commander. I told him I believed the corporal purposely put my life in danger in order to retaliate on behalf of my former partner. The captain responded, "Brandon, sounds like the corporal was only trying to gauge your ability to handle the situation. I'm sure he has a good reason for doing this."

I told the captain that no one officer would be expected to handle two large crowds of angry people. These folks were ready to engage in a neighborhood free-for-all. This incident could've easily ended in bloodshed or even homicide.

Sinful Enticement

Things weren't always bad while working in Garland as an officer. Here's an incident that took place a couple years earlier. Around 3:00 AM, the dispatcher broadcasted that a large group of people were fighting at the Waffle House (WH). My sergeant at the time was only a few blocks from there, so he was the first to arrive. I arrived within seconds after him. Through the large glass windowpane, I could see my sergeant fighting a disorderly club goer inside. He was highly intoxicated and refused to leave the restaurant.

I put my cruiser in park. Without delay, I jumped forcefully out of it, only to be slammed back into my seat. I had neglected to take off my seatbelt and nearly strangled myself to death with it when I tried to exit my car. By the time I made it to the entrance, my sergeant was hurling the suspect outside. I joined in the fight. *Boom, bam, pow* and a couple of *ka-bangs* later, the suspect stopped fighting. He was placed under arrest and escorted to the detention center for booking. The sergeant, several other officers, and I remained on scene to assist with crowd control. Roughly four or five hundred people flooded the parking lot. This was a usual occurrence every Friday, Saturday, and

Sunday night. Whenever the clubs closed, the WH became the after-party spot. The groups of people that were fighting fled the scene long before our arrival. We stood around the perimeter of the restaurant and instructed those who weren't patrons to leave the premises.

Within the crowd, we saw a team of strippers that traveled from Memphis. Some of them were also CSU and Truman University students. Whenever these ladies came around they were the topic of conversation. One stripper always seemed to catch the attention of everyone in the crowd, including the officers on scene. I had met her a month prior at her place of employment. A friend and I went to this hole in the wall strip club and saw some of the most despicable sights. We mostly laughed and poked fun at every stripper that worked there, but then Candy walked in.

"Wow! Do you see all that?"

"Hell yeah, I see her big booty ass. Damn man, she fine as hell."

Candy, quite simply, commanded the attention of everyone in her presence. She could have easily have been voted Miss whatever she chose to be. Candy looked very much like one of those perfectly shaped woman in the music videos, the cover of King Magazine or in a box office hit love scene. She was a brown-skinned, African-American queen. Her hair hung just below her shoulders. She had the most captivating eyes and bolstered an indescribable physique. She was about five-six, and her weight was around 140 pounds, distributed in *all* the right places.

The first night the officers and I saw this woman she was wearing, notably, a pair of high heel stilettos. She was clothed in an ensemble resembling the beautiful, Beyoncé's performance outfit during the 2011 Billboard Music Awards. Her dress landed slightly above the center of her thighs. It had fringes that ran up her thighs, and with each step they flung apart, revealing her lovely brown skin. One could easily see the inside of her upper thighs and the very lowest portion of cleavage. Her dress was revealing.

And again, we were hypnotized as Candy ripped the runway of the WH parking lot. "OMG," one of the officers jokingly said, "I don't particularly like black women but I think I'd make an exception for that lady." Her well-toned legs and sculpted body faded away into the crowd. "Damn, where did she go?"

A few weeks later, while working crowd control at the WH, we spotted this mystic beauty once again. I thought, *why would a woman as stunning as her want to be a stripper? Doesn't she realize that any man she'd give the chance to would gladly take care of her for the rest of her life?*

As my former pastor in Miami Springs, Florida would say when speaking about fornication, "Shawty is a ten, thicker than a snicker but in all the right places."

Candy spotted me and smiled as she was parking her vehicle. I stood there totally distracted. I was batting my eyes in an awkward manner like a corny school kid. She giggled once she saw how I responded. She drove past and parked in a nearby parking space. She called me over and whispered gently in my ear, "I want to spend some more of that police money," before she and her friend walked into the WH. Luckily, none of my coworkers heard her comment. They were too preoccupied gazing at her.

I made a mistake the night I met Candy. This mistake could've cost me my job and jail time. It happened the night I went to the strip club called the Boat. The club was named appropriately because it was an old structure shaped like a boat. I personally never cared to go to strip clubs for different reasons, the primary one being that it goes against God's word. I never went to a strip club prior to that night, and in my lifetime, I've visited a strip club less than five times.

Most of the strippers at the Boat were overweight. They looked more like retired NFL lineman rather than dancers. My first experience was my worst, or so I thought. The graphic images were unbearable. Many of them had stretch marks that ran across their bodies like interstates and highways on a road map. Some of the women looked tougher and meaner than the local thugs and drug dealers. I sure hadn't missed out on much. The strip club showcased black strippers, but there were quite a few white patrons milling about. They were scouting potential "partners". I saw an old white guy leave the club with one of the strippers for the obvious reasons.

"Can we do that? I thought that was only legal in Nevada?

My friend laughed and slapped me across the back as we took a seat at the bar. There were about three or four strippers from out-of-state and they were gorgeous. At most strip clubs, the out-of-town chicks are always the most attractive and popular. Candy stood out and I tried to get a lap dance from her. But too many people approached her wanting the same. A line began to form. "To hell with that. I'm not waiting in line for a lap dance." I walked towards the stage. Since the lap dance area wasn't enclosed, I sat down and watched Candy give an old white gentleman a lap dance. He blew several hundred dollars in tips on her performance.

Several shots and a few beers later, my friend and I called it a night. We walked out of the club. I told him this was my first and last time coming to a strip club. We laughed hard at this and got into his vehicle and drove away. At a red light three blocks away from the club we saw Candy. She was in a black SUV with several other strippers. We looked on. Their music blared. They talked loudly and tippled down their mixed drinks. I could smell their perfume from my friend's car. The light turned green and they drove away. My friend and I had a short dialogue about pursuing them. We concluded that we would follow them "...like an ox going to the slaughter...like a stag caught in a trap, awaiting the arrow that would pierce its heart..." (Proverbs 7:22)

We drove into a hotel parking lot behind them. Soon after, another carload of strippers pulled in. They got out of their vehicle and congregated together. Then someone turned on the radio and began to dance provocatively. They were hanging out in the parking lot. I exited the vehicle and leaned against it, scanning the crowd for Candy. I attempted to approach her as soon as I saw her, but I was intercepted by her manager. Okay! He was her pimp.

After he introduced us, and before he left to attend to the other ladies he gave us a room number. Candy and I walked into the dark room together. She didn't talk much, nor did I. She walked in wearing high heels and left wearing flats. She carried her stilettos in hand. And I left the hotel with a hundred dollars less than what I originally had.

It turned out that she attended school at the same university I did. We had several chanced meetings after that night and exchanged numbers. We crossed paths twice at the WH when I and a few other officers were directing traffic and conducting crowd control. Although we exchanged numbers, we only spoke once over the phone. We never had an encounter like the night I met her. Well there was this one time when she invited me over to her place and I told her I didn't have any money. Then she said, "Who cares." But, somehow, we lost touch after that. For my own sake, I'm glad we lost touch. I can't imagine being caught in a trap, waiting to have my heart pierced. I don't care how attractive the woman is. It's not worth it.

Calm in the Storm

One night, while patrolling in a residential area near Truman University, I observed a vehicle driving extremely slow, approximately 10 mph in a posted 25 mph zone. I initiated my overhead emergency lights to conduct a traffic stop. I gave the dispatcher my location, tag number of the vehicle, and advised it was occupied one time. The driver pulled over to the curb. I asked why he was driving so slowly. When I was speaking, I noticed his car was filled with smoke. It reeked of marijuana. The driver was a young African-American male. He stared at me with a dumbfounded look affixed to his face. You know, the 'deer in headlights' look. It was quite apparent that he was smoking weed.

I asked him, "Where is it? Give it to me, now. If you lie to me, you are going to jail. But if you're honest, I'll give you a break."

The kid pulled a quarter pound of weed ($200-$800 worth depending on quality) out of his coat pocket and said, "Here, here it is, officer."

by Brandon Williams

I definitely didn't think he had that much weed. Now I gave him the 'deer in headlights' look. I thought about giving the kid a break despite him producing more weed than I had originally expected. He was a senior at Truman and was graduating the following semester. If I arrest him, this would place a huge strain on all he had worked hard to accomplish. I've seen many of my white coworkers give even heftier breaks to white college students. Somehow, they always seemed to fall short of extending that same courtesy to minority students. I regularly arrested both black and white students indiscriminately. This would be my first time giving someone the "Get Out of Jail Free" card for a drug-related offense. I wanted to make sure there was equality in this so called "officer discretion".

I had told the kid I wouldn't arrest him if he were honest. He was honest. My word is bond. I despondently allowed him to go free. Before leaving the scene, I threw the weed into a nearby sewer. I'm sure the rodents and critters down there didn't know what hit them. I imagine they went into a euphoric, zombie-like binge after nibbling away the would-be evidence, running rampant and eating everything in their path. Later, they likely succumbed to a sudden feeling of drowsiness. Their memory had failed them while attempting to navigate their way back through the tunnels. Unforgiving, they slumbered where they were, in an unfamiliar part of the sewer.

Some time had passed when I received an unreasonably random kind act from a concerned citizen. I was working a traffic crash one evening at a busy intersection and it was raining abnormally hard. Cosmic size rain drops pounded against my tired, exhausted body. I felt like I was in the Vietnam War scene from the movie *Forest Gump*. Forest reflected on a rain storm, "One day it started raining, and it didn't quit for four months. We been through every kind of rain there is. Little bitty stingin' rain...and big ol' fat rain. Rain that flew in sideways. And sometimes rain even seemed to come straight up from underneath."

I was drenched. I couldn't get to my cruiser to retrieve my raincoat because I was directing traffic. The traffic signals in all four directions had malfunctioned because of the storm. I noticed my sergeant and Lieutenant, whom I hold a great deal of respect for, laughing at me. They were assisting on the scene wrapped in the comfort of their raincoats. A silver Cadillac approached me slowly, as if it were about to stop. I motioned for the driver to drive pass. The vehicle was several feet away when the driver rolled down the window. I looked intently inside the vehicle. Seated inside was a little, old white lady. She was well dressed and smelled of expensive perfume. Her white pearl earrings matched the pearl necklace that adorned her neck. She motioned me closer.

"Son, you need to get out of this rainstorm," she said with the same temperament as a mother expressing concern for her children. Her nice words were well received.

I smiled and paused shortly before responding, "I would love to Ma'am, but there's been a multiple car crash. One of the vehicles is disabled just north of this intersection. Right there," I pointed. "I will be here directing traffic until it is towed out of the roadway."

"That's unbelievable!" Officer, here, I have something for you." She said this while opening her door. Based on the scene Forest described, one can only imagine that at least two or three feet of water, at a bare minimum, poured into the old lady's car when she opened her door.

"Ma'am, it's okay. I appreciate your thoughtfulness but we can't accept gifts." I attempted to close her door shut to keep her from getting soaked or stung to death by those God awful "stingin" rain drops. But she insisted on giving me the gift and propped her hand against the door to prevent me from closing it. After a couple seconds of fumbling through her backseat, she handed me a silver umbrella. Wow, it matched her car. I was stunned by her compassion.

I took the umbrella and thanked her. She drove away smiling. I was overwhelmed with amazement because many of her peers wouldn't have done that. Normally, when someone stops to talk to the police, it's to complain, file a report or hurl insults and speed away. I was deeply moved and taken aback by the old woman's unusual act of kindness.

I would like to tell you about a dissimilar encounter several police officers and I experienced with another old lady. The officers and I responded to a prowler complaint in a well-to-do area of the city.

Upon arrival, we searched the perimeter of the residence. Other officers on the scene circulated the immediate area in their cruisers for possible suspects. A sergeant later arrived and spoke with the homeowner. The dispatcher advised she needed an officer to clear the scene and respond to another call for service. I decided to get 10-8 and answer that call. Before I did, I walked to the front door of the residence where my sergeant was interviewing the complainant to inform him that I was leaving. I stood behind him and waited for a pause. While I was standing there, the complainant, an old white lady, peeped out of the door and gazed at me. My sergeant turned around and looked back to see what had startled her. He turned to her after seeing me and asked her if something was wrong. She opened her eyes wider. Her body started shaking. She covered her mouth with one hand and said, "That's him. Sir, that's definitely him. He's the one."

I was in awe. Instantly, I began to reflect on the countless victims who were jailed, beaten, and killed because of these types of situations. Frustrated, my sergeant interrupted her.

by Brandon Williams

"Ma'am, are you saying he's the one who tried to break into your house?"

"Yes!" she exclaimed candidly.

Some of the officers who were canvassing her property rushed over once they heard the commotion. What an awful acting job. She wouldn't make it in Hollywood. Well, on second thought, maybe she would.

My sergeant asked her again after allowing her to get a succeeding look at me. But she maintained her position with certainty. I was the prowler. My sergeant placed his hand on my shoulder as he guided me from behind him to introduce us. "Ma'am, this is Officer Williams. He's one of my officers."

"Hello, nice meeting you," I said.

"Oh my! Oh my!" She looked at my uniform and badge. Shortly afterwards, she settled down and offered an apology. I told my Sergeant there was a call for service pending and that I was responding to it. In the same approach as a prowler, I scrambled away swiftly. I purposely left during her apology, being that I found it to be halfhearted and somewhat insulting.

Over the years at the Garland Police Department, I had come to learn a lot and discovered some things about myself. As a police officer, I was afforded the opportunity to interact with prostitutes, drug dealers, would-be killers and robbers, the homeless, battered woman, drunks, and addicts. They're the same kinds of people that helped raise me when I lived in the street with my mother as a child. I credit much of who I've become to the love I received in the street. It's amazing how a rose can grow from the concrete.

"Did you hear about the rose that grew from a crack in the concrete? Proving nature's law is wrong it learned to walk without having feet. Funny it seems, but by keeping its dreams, it learned to breathe fresh air. Long live the rose that grew from concrete when no one else ever cared." -2pac

Unlike many police officers across the country, I made sure to treat *everyone* with dignity and respect. I was able to help some get their lives back on the right track. One story in particular is about a young lady who was a victim of domestic violence. We attended the same university, CSU. Her boyfriend beat her unsparingly. He did this whenever he decided to. He took her car from her and ransacked her apartment, none of which he was financially vested. It was heart-wrenching the nights I was called out to her apartment. I once witnessed her at the height of her young, fun-filled romantic life when she had dated a good friend whose model football jock life was cut short by the hands of a drunk driver in a head-on collision. Now that he had passed away, she was trapped within a bottomless valley of counterfeit-love. This is the breeding ground for abuse, betrayal, and our darkest fears.

It took a while, but after many conversations she decided to leave. Luckily enough for her, she did. Her cunning and abusive lover became a crack addict. Before this he was a crack dealer. Notwithstanding the powerful blows crack threw at him, his life began to fall apart. To her credit, she left him shortly after the onset of his addiction. Otherwise, he would have introduced her to his new habit. In many cases the companion would have several choices: Smoke crack with her lover willingly to prove their love or get beaten or coerced into smoking it. Unfortunately, being forced to use drugs or to have sex with other men by your abuser isn't the worst that can happen to you. Not even death. I believe the worst is seeing that same abuse fall onto your helpless children.

Throughout the years I've interviewed and come in contact with many addicts and their families, a common thread is that the addict would loan out his or her children to sexual predators in exchange for crack or their drug of choice. In some cases, the children would be as young as three and four years old.

Let's stand up ladies and be women. Be the fearless and prevailing vessels God has created you to be. "It's not so bad," you say. "He didn't hold a gun to my head and make me do it." Stop pretending to be someone you're not. The words "it's not so bad," a bloody nose and swollen shut eyes don't pair well together.

I remember speaking to a prostitute, drug addict once. She told me she didn't want to live anymore. The pressures of life had taken the little hope she hung on to that her lifestyle didn't dissipate. After chatting with her for a while and sharing some personal stories, she cheered up. I told her an old saying of mine: No matter how hard life hits you, don't stop fighting back. Don't lean against the ropes and allow it to pound away at you. I reasoned, if life is hard—and it is—we don't have any other option but to keep trying. Quitting won't make the pain go away. It only prolongs and intensifies it.

She regained focus and said she was going in for the night. Although I do not know how much of an impact I had on her, I'm optimistic years later that she is alive and well today.

I became active in the high crime areas as a police officer and through outreach with a local church. I realized the passion I held for helping people was greater than what I initially thought it to be. I soon became so preoccupied with my aspirations of becoming a public speaker, sharing my story and experiences, I couldn't focus on anything other than that. I used to spend countless hours studying in various libraries across the city. This was highly unusual for me. I read material on the works of Mahatma Gandhi, Dr. Martin L. King, and my long-time hero Frederick Douglass, and many alike. I hoped to someday make a living as a public speaker and activist like the great people I read about.

During that time, I started a pre-owned car dealership, Cars-Plus, when I was twenty-four. I named it Cars-Plus because I had a vision to start a wrecking yard and a detail shop hence the 'Plus'. When I started the business I didn't have an objective for future growth. I didn't have prior business experience other than selling crack.

I was now running a business and my momma was very proud. Making sure to sell my entire inventory at the lowest price, I always disclosed any issues or defects my vehicles might have had. It was a lovely thing to be able to do something for the underprivileged and earning a fair wage while doing so. I became fascinated with the idea of being *Boss* and the grades I received in school suffered because of it. Within a year of starting the dealership, I was placed on academic probation and faced a hard decision. I had to quit the police department, close my business, or drop out of school. I wasn't happy with any of those options but I knew I couldn't resign from the police department. I had only had the business for a year. Although it turned a decent profit, I didn't feel comfortable relying on it as a primary source of income. And, being in my junior year, I had come too far in college to quit. With this in mind, I reluctantly decided to close the dealership.

During the year I had my business, I gained many cherished memories, one of which occurred at an auction in Jackson, Mississippi. It happened when the staff separated the owners and salesmen. The salesmen worked for the owners by buying inventory at the auction. The owners sometimes accompanied their salesmen to the auction and, at times, the salesmen went alone. The auction staff instructed the owners to stand on one side of the auction line and the salesmen on the other so they could drive their fleet between the two lines to be auctioned off. I noticed a large group of sixty-plus, primarily black, move to the salesmen line. Remaining on the owner's side was a small group of ten to fifteen men, comprised of old, wealthy white men. I was intimidated. I thought, *I can't stand here with these guys.* Then I proceeded to make way to the salesmen side. Until a rude staff member approached me.

"Sir, is everything okay? All of the salesmen are to stand there. You appear to be a little confused. Here, let me help you." He placed his hand on my back and guided me to the salesmen line. Some of his colleagues appeared to be laughing.

Stopping, I sarcastically thanked the guy and insisted that I was in the appropriate line. I walked back to the all-white club of owners and stood in line with them. Some of them greeted me. They asked about my dealership to get an idea of my worth and ability to compete with them. They used a sort of unfamiliar language.

by Brandon Williams

"Do you have a floor plan?"

"A floor plan? What on earth is a floor plan?"

"It's a credit line for dealerships to buy vehicles."

I smiled and laughed when I felt it appropriate, like a new student trying hard to fit in. The staff that asked me to leave the owner's line came back with another gentleman demanding to see my credentials. He didn't require this of any of my peers. I showed him my documentation and sent him on his way. Later on in the day, I noticed a young black guy who was also an owner. He looked to be in his mid-thirties. We admired one another's position. He offered me some encouraging words and a few pointers. He had been in business since he was my age. We exchanged numbers and continued on our way. I went on to purchase a vast commercial lot for additional business ventures. It was roughly four acres, situated in a densely populated area.

After closing the dealership, I was able to focus on school. The following semester, I got off academic probation.

It was in late August of 2005 when the most destructive and costliest natural disaster in the history of this country touchdown in Louisiana. Hurricane Katrina claimed the lives of more than 1800 people, over 1500 of them killed in Louisiana. America's biggest disaster to date, Hurricane Sandy, reportedly claimed the lives of less than 300 people. It was estimated that the total economic impact in

Louisiana and Mississippi may exceed $150 billion, nearly three times more than Sandy. Almost 900,000 people in Louisiana lost power as a result of Katrina. It was reported that 80 percent of New Orleans was under water. Hopefully, most of us are aware of the poor response and lack of leadership on the part of the government to provide relief. With over 65 percent of the city's population being African-American, many believed that race and class contributed to the delays in government response.

President Bush received criticism from rap superstar Kanye West during a concert for hurricane relief. West said, "George Bush doesn't care about black people." West's comment became widely popular as it expressed the views of many black Americans. More than anyone, the victims of hurricane Katrina felt this way. Bush was also criticized for not immediately returning to Washington from his vacation in Texas after the hurricane hit. After sharp criticism televised across the world, relief aids poured in and President Bush finally paid a visit to the Gulf Coast and was briefed on Katrina. There were many false reports of rapes, murders, carjacking and other violent crimes. The media played on this.

Although some of my family members may have suffered damaged or destroyed property, I thanked God since none of them lost their lives. I was living in Garland and attended college in Midland during Katrina. Located in the east-central region of Tennessee, Garland wasn't affected too much by the hurricane, minus heavy rain. Residents from all over south Louisiana, primary the N.O. area, evacuated to Garland. They hoped to find shelter and aid. Times were hard and I constantly worried about my relatives who lived in south Louisiana. I was on the phone every hour with them for updates. I told them they could stay with me if they needed to.

As a result of the number of evacuees in Garland, I wasn't able to take off work to visit my family during the storm. In addition, most of the highways and interstates where my relatives lived were closed. Therefore, my personal experiences with Katrina are limited to what I experienced as a police officer and the stories I heard from family and friends. I have many memoires and thoughts that trouble me regarding the hurricane, but there are a few that stood out more than others. Many of the white residents within the city started spreading rumors about the people that recently evacuated from the N.O. area. It was said that the "refugees" were targeting the local residents and committing crimes against them. These complaints came chiefly from the citizens on the north side of town, which was a predominately well-to-do white area. One of the widespread rumors was that a couple of refugees raped and killed a well-known white woman from the north side of town. Another was that they robbed and murdered a business man who was highly regarded. These rumors started to spark racial tension within the city, and even within the police department. I believe that was the purpose and the motive of the people who started the rumors.

I was in the office one day answering 911 calls when a white woman called in a complaint regarding the "refugees". I asked the caller what her emergency was and she stated, "There are about two of them walking down the street, pushing a bicycle."

"Two of what, Ma'am?" I carefully asked.

"Two of them refugees from N.O." she exclaimed! When asked, she was unable to say what crime the two gentlemen had committed other than pushing a bicycle down the street while black.

We received countless 911 calls similar to this one. In a comparable call, a complainant expressed his concerns about the horrible people from south Louisiana who were now populating his city. When I told the complainant that I had relatives who were from Louisiana, he justified his statement by saying, "Well, not all of them are bad. Some are okay, like your family."

I walked into the dispatcher's office one day while several of my coworkers was on the phone. They were talking to an officer or state trooper from our area. He was sent to N.O. after the governor declared a state of emergency. The officer was boasting about a black guy he had killed in N.O. Upon hearing this, my colleagues were enraged. They were stricken with an unparalleled envy because they weren't sent to

Louisiana. I suppose they wanted so badly to kill a few blacks. The officer continued to share his highly coveted story. My coworkers griped about our chief not sending them to N.O. Their rants were reflective of their hatred for black people.

With all of the devastation the people affected by Katrina faced, there were police officers having a tantrum because they couldn't harass or kill them. Such officers could get away with using excessive force, causing severe injury and murdering residents of N.O. Police officers were allegedly authorized to shoot looters. In addition, N.O. was blanketed with a thick cloud of chaos and panic, among many other distractions, those officers used to their advantage.

Henry Glover, a thirty-one year old African-American local from the Aligers community of New Orleans was shot to death by a police officer. Henry's corpse was set on fire during the officer's effort to conceal his murder. One of the officers on scene assaulted an eyewitness who tried to help Henry prior to his murder. His scorched corpse was reduced to ashes, burnt flesh, and bone fragments. His body or what remained of it was ultimately discovered in the car he was incinerated in.

Let's not forget about the Danziger Bridge massacre in N.O. Two unarmed man were killed by officers wielding an assault rifle and a shotgun. One of the men the police murdered was stomped repeatedly in the back by an officer before he passed away. Several other unarmed people were wounded by the officers.

There are countless stories similar to these detailing police misconduct following the aftermath of Katrina. A few of these stories received some attention from the media, but many went untold.

Have a good one, boys. I walked out of the office unnoticed. Their hearts were in N.O. The smell of death was in the air and it aroused them. They are the police officers working in your community. They are entrusted to act impartially, absent of any racism and bias.

I was baffled when the media and locals, including officers, referred to the evacuees as "refugees". A refugee is someone who has been forced to leave their country in order to escape war, persecution, or natural disaster. Merriam-Webster defines it as: One that flees; especially: a person who flees to a foreign country or power to escape danger or persecution. I corrected many people until I realized that most of them were intentionally calling the victims of the hurricane "refugees". Upon learning this, my distain for senseless hatred grew even stronger.

I patrolled the areas where the evacuees were housed throughout the city of Garland. I visited all of the shelters and offered encouraging words to some of them. Most of the people there were resilient and very optimistic about their futures, in spite of their current circumstances. I met a lot of fabulous people from N.O. and even gained a friend. We keep in touch even today. The sad thing is that I've also lost contact with a lot of my friends from N.O. I'm not sure if they were killed or displaced. I still carry the hope of seeing them again.

One of Garland's main shelters was located inside the Civic Center. This is where I met a phenomenal woman named Catherine Knight. Ms. Knight treated everyone housed at the Civic Center with the greatest respect and hospitality one could imagine. Unlike most of the people in a position to help the evacuees, she poured all of her energy into ensuring that everyone's needs were met. She didn't leave a stone unturned. She far exceeded what her duties required of her.

One night, as tensions heightened at the Civic Center, as they did from time to time, there was a young mother of two arguing with another evacuee. The mother was the apparent aggressor. I rushed over and separated the two, reminding the young mother that her behavior affects everyone in the shelter. She was very angry. I was certain; if I had not intervened she would have attacked the other woman. Later that night, I witnessed the same young mother yelling and screaming at Ms. Knight. I ran over to stop the altercation but Ms. Knight insisted on hearing the woman out. I stood there as this lady scolded Ms. Knight and accused her of not caring for the evacuees. At the end of this arsenal of verbal attacks, Ms. Knight discovered the root of the problem. The young mother wanted Ms. Knight to apply for jobs for her. She refused to apply for jobs herself. She wasn't handicapped or anything. She just didn't want to apply for jobs herself. She wanted Ms. Knight to apply for jobs on her behalf.

At the Civic Center, those that were displaced received shelter, food, counseling, and medical treatment. Apart from this, the only other pertinent service provided was job search assistance. Evacuees were introduced to participating employers that had openings. Ms. Knight made computers available for those that wished to search for local as well as out-of-town jobs. But filling out a job application for someone who was quite able to do so for herself wasn't an offered service.

After the showdown in the middle of the Civic Center, I walked Ms. Knight to her office. She was devastated by the woman's hurtful insults and began to question if she could do more. I never knew Ms. Knight before that, day but I have never seen anyone in Garland, black or white, express this level of care about the evacuees in our area. I told Ms. Knight not to let the woman's hurtful words get her down. I planned to speak to my sergeant and have the young woman placed in another shelter, or possibly arrested if she continued causing problems with other evacuees.

Ms. Knight disagreed. "We'll find another way to keep the environment in order without removing or arresting the woman." She cited that the young woman had two kids who wouldn't have a place to go.

by Brandon Williams

Months later, things started to get better for the people who evacuated to Garland. Many of them finally received their insurance claims, government aid, and family help. Some moved to Houston, Dallas, and Atlanta, while others chose to return to Louisiana. Some decided to stay in Garland and set out to rebuild everything they lost.

Officer Friendly

I was on the scene of a crash where two wreckers responded to tow the same car. One of the wreckers was called to the scene and the other came uninvited. A lieutenant I was working with spoke to the wrecker operator that wasn't summoned to the scene. He was asked to leave. The operator refused, claiming that he would be towing the disabled vehicle. He became very loud and yelled at the lieutenant. A couple of other officers were on the scene but didn't seem to notice. I decided to walk over and assist the lieutenant.

When I got close enough, the lieutenant whispered something to me. He asked if I knew who the irate operator was.

"No, I do not. Is he someone I should know?"

"He is the Grand Dragon of the area Klu Klux Klan. I went to school with him back in the day." A Grand Dragon is supposedly the highest ranking Klansman in a given state. "Brandon you can 'lay hands on him' if you want to. He has been ordered to leave twice and that's only one of the charges we have on him."

I looked the man over carefully, expecting to see much more for a so called Grand Dragon, or "Grand Lizard" as some of my white co-workers jokingly called him. Some officers stood by and waited for my response. I thought about it briefly. Lawfully kicking this racist's ass had a unique appeal. But I decided not to take advantage of the situation or his stupidity.

I had been involved in many fights as an officer. I wasn't afraid to fight. That earned me a wealth of respect from my peers. Even from those who disliked me. The lieutenant counted on me barking out an order to which the "Grand Lizard", operator would've refused, thus granting me free reign. I'm sure hundreds, if not thousands, of minorities across the country would have purchased tickets and stood in line for that opportunity. But I took the oath. I swore to protect. This even means protecting a man who would take my life simply because of my race. Without trickery, I walked over to him and asked him to leave. He did so immediately.

I received a call for service late one night in reference to a man walking in the street. He was impeding the flow of traffic, nearly causing an accident. The dispatcher advised the man was a black male draped in a white sheet, wearing only a red Speedo. The suspect had a long history of mental health problems. The complainant stated that the suspect claimed to be the Savior. He told the complainant he was Jesus Christ of Nazareth, and he was walking to Bethlehem.

Once I arrived on the scene, I saw the suspect walking out of the roadway onto the sidewalk. He was approximately six-two in height and weighed somewhere around two-hundred and fifty pounds with an athletic build. This guy was huge and he was, by far, one of the strangest sights I'd seen for the day. I parked my cruiser and got out to speak with him. I made contact and asked him what he was doing.

"Nothing," he replied, while attempting to walk past me.

I stood in front of him and ordered him to stop. I asked for his name and supporting identification to validate his identity. He was in a full sweat; it was apparent that he had been walking for a while.

He said, "My name is Jesus Christ and I am on my way to Bethlehem." Then, out of nowhere, a gust of wind blew open his sheet.

"Cover yourself. Jesus Christ! Are you really the Christ?" "Yes, it is I."

I was amused but I became impatient as passing motorists began driving recklessly because they were so busy looking at him instead of the roadway.

"Okay Jesus Christ, place your hands behind your back. You're going to jail." I reached for my handcuffs and the guy pleaded for me not to arrest him.

"Officer, don't take me to jail."

"I have to get you somewhere safe. How else can I keep you from walking in the middle of the street naked?" I paused for a second. I thought about giving him a break. But I couldn't do that unless he produced a valid name and information where I could contact his family. I asked him once more for his name and where he was going. He maintained that his name was Jesus Christ of Nazareth and that he was walking to Bethlehem.

I grabbed his arm and pulled it behind his back to place my handcuffs on him.

"Oh, no, Officer, my name is Terry Dunn."

"I thought you told me your name was Jesus Christ and you were walking to Bethlehem."

"No Sir, my name is Terry Dunn and I am walking to the Church of Bethlehem to praise Jesus Christ. I just got caught up in the spirit," he exclaimed.

To keep from laughing, I continued to be upset. He told me where his mother lived. I placed him in my cruiser and drove him to her house. She was also his caregiver. After I dropped him off, I laughed until my stomach ached. That guy was hilarious.

Weeks after the 'Jena Six' incident in December of 2006, a good friend of mine found a noose hanging from her carport. This terrified the single mother of four who was also a Katrina evacuee that chose to stay in Garland with the hopes of starting a new life. The term 'Jena Six' was coined when six black students had a fight with a white student at school. Although, the white student only sustained minor injury the black students were charged with attempted murder. The incident sparked racial tension in the town of Jena, Louisiana and surrounding areas. The school the students attended was 90 percent white and 10 percent black, which reflected the town's population. My friend, a beautiful lady from Honduras, moved to New Orleans at a young age, where she grew up. When she called me crying, she was so upset and frantic, I could hardly understand what she was trying to tell me. I drove over to her house and found her sitting outside on her steps, crying. I walked up to her and she pointed towards her carport, saying, "Look."

I continued looking in the direction she pointed until I saw the noose. It was hanging down from a wooden beam underneath her carport. An extreme display of violence, hatred, and ignorance is what this symbolized. I sat there with my friend as she cried, and I said nothing. For the first time, I couldn't think of anything to say. We sat together until some of her friends from a local church arrived to console her. Her friends attended the same church where one of the pastors inquired if my friend and I were romantically involved. The pastor told my friend not to bring me back to their church. He had an issue with the attractive Honduran native dating a black man.

Before I left I told her I would constantly check on her and her kids throughout the night. I kept my word. I patrolled the area as frequently as I could in between responding to calls for service, taking reports and making arrests. Honestly, her home was outside Garland city limits and I didn't have police powers there. But the perpetrator was later caught and convicted in federal court. He was sentenced to one year in a federal prison for the federal hate crime. He admitted in court that he hung the noose to send a message to the African-American males that visited my friend's home. His statement caused me to wonder if this lunatic had been stalking her, and if he conspired to do more damage than hanging the noose. My friend has since recovered and hasn't experienced anything remotely similar to this hateful act.

The Delta in Red (Dir) surprised me one night at work, when she was thought to be in San Diego, California visiting family. Dir and I became acquainted when I worked a security detail at her bank. During that time, many banks near the I-40 corridor were being robbed. Therefore, her bank, exercising wisdom, hired off-duty policemen for security. We soon discovered that we attended the same university (CSU), and that we had a friend in common. Once, she called me while on-duty.

"Hey Brandon, what are you up to?"

"I been busting my ass all day, call after call. You know how that goes. How was your trip? You're coming back in the morning, right?"

"Yes, I'll be back in town tomorrow morning, and I can't wait to see you!" She laughed before a brief pause.

"Same here. I'll see you once you make it back." I radioed to the dispatcher, "Cruiser 1865 to Garland."

"Go ahead Cruiser 1865."

"I'll be out at my residence for a 10-32 (lunch break)."

"Are you on break? Hum…how long is your break?"

"Normally thirty minutes if I don't get a call and then lunch is over. Why?"

"Well, I was thinking about bringing you something to eat."

"Really? That would be fine if you were actually here, woman, now stop playing with me," I laughed. "I'll talk with you later. I'm about to grab a bite to eat."

"Call me whenever you can. Take care."

I exited my cruiser and walked into my apartment. Looking through my empty refrigerator for something to eat, I stood there, puzzled, as if I hadn't already known it was empty.

Knock, knock.

The sound was coming from my front door. They knocked again. "Damn, who is it?" I mumbled while walking to the door. This better not be my neighbor who always borrowed things and never returned them. I opened my door quickly to startle him. Shouting, "Man, what do you need now?"

It wasn't him.

"Surprise!"

"Wow! Really! Have you been here since you called me?"

It was Dir, standing in my doorway, wearing a tan belted trench coat. The stunning pair of red high heels she wore complimented her trench coat well. She smelled as good as she looked. She had my undivided attention. Walking up to me, she extended herself on the tips of her toes and wrapped her arms around my neck. She pressed her body tightly against mine and greeted me with the most intimate kiss. As we kissed, I cradled the lower portion of her derrière and lifted her off her feet. I put her down and asked about her trip.

Rushing back to the kitchen, I scrambled to find something to eat while we discussed her trip. I looked back across the room at Dir. She was standing in my living room, unfastening the belt of her trench coat. "Babes, are you going to stay here because I have to leave in about twenty-five minutes. The key is on the counter." I heard the sound of her coat falling to the floor.

"Do you have time to eat the dinner I brought for you?"

I looked up from the kitchen counter and was amazed. Dir's well-toned and sculpted body from years of being on the university's dance team hypnotized me. She left little to the imagination in her ravishing, red lace bra and panties. She looked very much like Jet Magazine's beauty of the month.

She walked to the center of my living room and posed. My eyes bounced back and forth from her nice smile, breasts, panties, and those red heels. Straightaway, I led Dir into the Lion's den to be devoured. Dir asked me to sit on the edge of the bed while keeping my feet on the floor. Then she told me to lie back horizontally, and I did. Standing between my legs and turning her back to me, she positioned her legs between mine, using them for support. She placed her hands on my thighs for balance as she sat down atop of me. She clutched my thighs firmly. She moved her waist back and forth in a circular motion, riding it in reverse. I believe that's the day Dir and I broke my bed.

I ate the dinner she brought me. It was succulent. All too soon, the dispatcher radioed, "Garland to Cruiser 1865."

"Go ahead Garland," I responded.

"What's your 10-20 (Location)?"

"I'm at home, finishing up dinner." I looked over at a sleepy and exhausted Dir, who was laughing at me.

"10-4 (acknowledgement). Well, I have a couple of calls pending."

"Copy that. I'm 10-8 (in service or available for calls)." I fumbled with my stubborn duty belt while trying to put it back on.

Performing oral sex on a girlfriend while she was driving down the interstate was one of the most 'out of the box' things I ever did sexually. One day, we were talking about how guys liked having their mate perform oral sex on them, among other fantasies. I told her about a friend who said his girlfriend gave him a "head job" for his birthday while he was driving them to dinner. She asked what I thought about my friend's birthday gift. I replied, "Best ever!" She started smiling and jokingly said that she wanted to share that experience with me. And we did.

I told her that same day that I'd like to return the favor. She said it would be too complicated and much harder for me to perform oral sex on her while she was driving. But it really wasn't. We were driving back to Garland from visiting some of her family in Atlanta. I put my hands between her legs and started caressing her. One thing led to another and the next thing I knew, we were weaving and swerving down the freeway. We frequently crossed the yellow line and drove onto the ridges on the shoulder of the road that makes the loud roaring noise when you drive on them.

"There's someone driving next to us babe. I think they can see us. Babe! They, can, see, us!" she said each time I kissed, licked, and sucked, her panic button. She eventually pulled over to the shoulder of the road to recoup. She looked over at me and, with a huge smirk on her face, and told me I was crazy.

Reality of Life's Lessons

〜

I'm paying the cost of living a sinful lifestyle. I engaged in a sexual fling with an older woman that an old friend of mine slept with. The woman was looking for more than sex and purposely got pregnant. She did so with hopes of forcing me into a relationship with her. In addition to taking care of my unborn child, she tried to persuade me to take care of her and her other three kids. I got a reality check when this happened. But I can't blame the opportunistic woman who seized the moment. I blame myself and take full responsibility. I blamed myself for not taking appropriate precaution to prevent things like this from happening. I thought I was craftier than her. I remember the last time I had unprotected sex with her; she originally told me she wasn't ovulating. She was adamant when saying she couldn't get pregnant during that phase. When we were done, she asked if I had ejaculated inside of her. This was my first time becoming suspicious. She said in the most unconvincing way, "I may get pregnant. I didn't know you came." I remained silent and startled. It was apparent that she was trying to trap me. I had only known her for about three weeks. I walked away laughing at her. I was done with this woman before she got me caught up. Close call, or so I thought.

The basis of our association was purely sexual, and she was fully aware and claimed to be in agreement with that. I'm not sure how well memory serves me, but I think she called me about two or three hours later and told me she was pregnant. Okay, maybe several days passed when she told me, but it felt like minutes. I was in a miserable state. I couldn't stomach the thought of having a child with a woman I didn't know. To make matters worse, by a woman many would refer to as a whore. She was excited and hopeful that her efforts would earn her a relationship with me. She talked about having an abortion by some other guy she had a fling with, and said she would get another if she ever got pregnant again.

I became depressed because I realized that many of the hardships in my life as an adult were self-inflicted. I took responsibility for my behavior. There are countless women out there today that prey on men, hoping for the right one to save them. We all know there's a handful of men out there doing the same thing. Purposely getting pregnant or getting someone pregnant won't change the reality of who you are. Or the way someone views you.

I thought about the women who are raped and conceive children. I wondered how they feel about sharing a child with someone and having no choice. I lost contact with her once she realized getting pregnant didn't make me want to be with her and father her children.

I told her I would provide for my child, but that I couldn't afford to take care of her whole family.

Almost a year passed before I found out that I had a daughter. I fell instantly in love with my precious little angel and became the father to her that every child needs. A father that is caring, loving, and consistent. Over the years, out of spite and ignorance, my daughter's mother would make it difficult for me to have a healthy relationship with my daughter. But I haven't allowed the "baby mamma drama" to faze me. I'm determined to stay in my daughter's life as long as I have breath in my lungs.

It seems my love for my daughter disappoints her mother. I believe, once she realized that having a child for me didn't earn her the relationship she had hoped for, she didn't care much about me having a relationship with my child.

I can imagine how multiple men calling her to check on their children causes problems in her current relationships. It seems like I mainly get to talk to my daughter when her mother is in between relationships. The latter proved true with my son's mother. I received a text from her telling me I couldn't talk to my son on certain days because it caused an inconvenience to her, my son, and her third husband.

Ladies and gentleman we all have a lot of things in our past that we are not proud of, but our shame doesn't excuse us from our responsibility. We have to own our mistakes and learn from them. I observed a similar pattern between my son and daughter mother's. Whenever they are dating, they create distance between my children and me. But when they're between relationships or marriages, they seem to be supportive. Children should be left out of the drama. Our children need two loving parents, no matter how much one may hate the other. If I, as a father, don't watch over my children, who will? Will it be the drug user my daughter's mother once dated? Will it be another man whose own children are in the same predicament? Who will be a father to our children, us or them? Who is parenting our children?

But who is at fault, me or the women I share children with? Surely we would all like to think the problem lays elsewhere. We shouldn't have to look any further than ourselves to see the person responsible for our situations.

My son is more fortunate than his little sister because his mother is a working class woman who I believe strides to meet his needs. However, the relationships that parents have with one another affects our children greatly. I still remember the day my son said, "Daddy's stupid and I hate Ms. Ashley." He was four years old at the time and he said that after not receiving something he wanted. He was riding his plastic push motorcycle. He rode it into the corner of my living room when he said it. That hurt badly.

Unmistakably, *Daddy's stupid and I hate Ms. Ashley* were his mother's words. I walked over to my son and hugged him while fighting back tears. I told him that Daddy isn't stupid and that daddy will always love him, no matter what someone may say.

I also received a disturbing text message from my son's mother. I'm sure she intended on sending it to someone else. The message read, "Jordan daddy just popped up out of nowhere and he claims he wants to see Jordan, girl, so Jordan going to be with him today." I always knew she talked against me but once she started dating other guys and got married a few times, I had hoped her focus would shift from me to them. By this time, my son was about five or six. His mother was running an endless campaign against me, slandering my credibility as a father, and my love for my son. It was clear that she aimed to not only discredit me to my child, but draw sympathy from others, too.

The strangest thing is, whenever we spoke, she was always polite. I wouldn't have ever thought she was so resentful and jealous of my relationship with my son. I love my son and daughter. No one will succeed in convincing them otherwise. I don't think of myself as a victim, nor do I feel sorry about what I'm experiencing. I take responsibility for the role I played in creating this situation for myself. In my mother's words, "boy, I bet you weren't worrying about how crazy those women were when you were in the bed with them." The sad truth is, she's right, I wasn't. I only cared about the few seconds of pleasure I received. I never thought seconds of pleasure would turn into a lifetime of pain. Although, in the end, I have found an immeasurable joy in my two beautiful, smart and healthy kids.

Through countless testimonies and interviews from various women over the years, I have come to know the pain a woman has to endure when sharing a child with a foolish man, as well. The story I chose to share stands out the most. It is the story of a single mother of two. She tried to work out child support arrangements with her children's father without involving the court. Her reason was because the father of her children threatened not to take part in their lives if she filed a child support suit in court. Once the two of them reached an agreement, he never honored the child support agreement as planned. In the long run, the mother found herself in dire straits and in desperate need of cash to provide for her kids. She told him about her situation. He agreed to bring her a child support payment right away. This would be his first time making a child support payment. Once he arrived at her house, he placed the money on the dresser in her bedroom. He even spent time with the kids he so often neglected. She was delighted to see this rare moment and thanked him for it. Before he left her home, he grabbed her and kissed her on the lips. She asked if he had lost his mind. Shortly afterwards, she told him to leave.

Quite some time had passed between their split and he had recently married. But before he left, he walked into her bedroom, took the money off the dresser and proceeded towards the front door. She tried to stop him from leaving with the money. There was only one thing she could do to make him give it back. Sex, he demanded sex in exchange for the child support payment for his kids. She refused and he left.

The trouble is, after that point, she did have sex with him for the payments. This became a regular occurrence. Whenever he came over with his child support payment she would have sex with him. She tried to convince herself that her new agreement wasn't that bad, but there was no denying it. She tried to talk him out of having sex with her by reminding him about his beautiful and loving wife he had at home. But that tactic never worked and he persisted on keeping their new agreement. He enjoyed bringing over his child support payment and having sex. She said she was broke and he provided the help she needed to make ends meet.

He would ask her to be dressed in lingerie when he came over and, at times, made her perform oral sex. He never missed a visit. After a time, however, she stopped allowing him to take advantage of her, and she filed for the child support suit. I wish she would've told his wife but she chose not to. She reasoned that he would continue sleeping around and his wife would eventually find out.

What a sad story. Hopefully all of us can learn from it. In many ways, it is better to learn from the testimonies of others rather than experience.

After a while, I resigned from Garland Police and accepted a position with the Davis Police Department. The Davis Police Department was known for being involved in police pursuits and shootouts. One of my friends, a lieutenant who worked there, offered me a position once he got word I put in my resignation letter with Garland Police. I had lots of good times in Davis working as a police officer. The residents of Davis were similar to the north Garland residents. There were many racists. The alienated relationships between blacks and whites paralleled the Jim Crow era. Somehow everyone managed to live together peacefully, but separately. I heard many horrible stories from black and white officers. One story was about a group of white officers who worked at a local police department within our county. The officers arrested and beat an innocent black man. Afterwards, they placed a black bag over his head and took pictures with him. They posed with big smiles, as if they were posing for a picture with a celebrity.

Another time, a Davis officer showed me a segregated grave site. Blacks were buried on the south end of the cemetery and whites were buried on the north side. A fence that ran down the middle of the cemetery divided it into two sections. This left me believing there was hatred amongst the dead as well as the living. Being a southerner, I'm no stranger to racism, but I was unaware that things like segregated grave yards still existed.

I recall responding to a scene to assist some paramedics at a residence with a disorderly crowd of teens. Upon arrival, I spoke with a teenager who said she was pregnant and wasn't feeling well. There were about five other teenagers between the ages of fourteen and seventeen that accompanied her. All of them appeared to be intoxicated, including the teen who said she was pregnant.

I got the rowdy crowd of teens settled in no time and assisted the medics with getting the pregnant teen into the ambulance. I asked the teens if there were any adults present. They pointed a few yards away to a trailer house. I walked over to the trailer and made contact with a couple of highly intoxicated adults. The drunken parents of the pregnant teen staggered to the door to greet me.

"What the hell is going on here, Officer…? Baby, did you call the police?"

"No I didn't call the cops. What's going on, Officer?"

"Your daughter is in the ambulance and she is about to be transported to the hospital because of pregnancy complications."

"Officer, ain't nothing wrong with that bitch. She always claims she's pregnant. I'm telling you, she does that shit to get attention."

They rushed passed me, the mother nearly falling while walking down the steps. They stormed towards the ambulance. I radioed a second time for the dispatcher to send another unit for assistance. I pursued them to the ambulance. As I approached, they opened the rear door of the ambulance. The paramedics attempted to stop the irate parents from entering the ambulance while they were rendering medical treatment to their teen daughter. I asked the medics to step aside and ordered the couple to stop, but they persisted. I attempted to close the rear door and was knocked against the ambulance when they snatched the door from me. I grabbed the father by his arm and escorted him away from his wife, placing him under arrest. Going back, I wrestled the mother out of the ambulance and attempted to calm her. However, once she realized that I arrested her husband, she became increasingly irate.

I continually called for additional officers for assistance. The group of teens started pacing franticly around me. They wanted to intervene. The drunken mother yelled and screamed at her daughter, and tried to get her out of the ambulance. I grabbed her arm to handcuff her and then her robe flung open, distastefully bearing all.

The medics looked as startled as I did. I released her arm, told her to close her robe, and put on some clothes. She was completely unclothed underneath. Once I let her go, she closed her robe and continued to yell obscenities at her daughter. She walked back to the ambulance again. I stopped her by grabbing her arm and, once more, she was partially disrobed. She became aggressive with me and tried to break free, attempting to jerk her arm away. I fought with her briefly. Eventually, I had her pinned against my car and handcuffed. During that time, the group of drunken teens was shouting for me to let her go. They were awaiting the opportune time to help the drunken woman. The backup I had been calling for, who was only seconds away, finally arrived twenty minutes later. I placed the woman in the assisting officer's cruiser and had the husband in mine. They were escorted to the police station and booked. Wrestling down a drunken, middle-aged, naked, white woman in that area was the last thing a black officer could ever imagine doing.

The nights I spent driving at high rates of speed in unmarked cars with the narcotics officers were very dangerous but exciting. In a fully loaded, white Ford F-150 with the aroma of 'new car' scent in the air, we led a caravan of officers to execute a high risk search warrant. Jay-Z and Linkin Park Numb/Encore blared as we approached the location listed on the warrant. Everyone transmitted something to the effect of, "Hey guys, let's do this," or "I'm locked and loaded, let's do this," over the radio to signal readiness. I gave the officer I was riding with a fist bump for good luck and silently said a prayer for our safety.

Once we arrived at our destination, everyone jumped out of their vehicles instantaneously. Pumped full of adrenaline, I grabbed my seventy pound "bitch" police breaching ram, and was the first to exit. I ran through a ditch, around some hedges and sprinted to the front door of our target location. Other officers armed with assault rifles had the house surrounded. I reared back my bitch and vigorously thrust it forward. I struck the door alongside of its knob. *Boom*, and the door burst open! I heard the sounds of footsteps raiding the suspect's home.

"Police, police, search warrant! Search warrant!" I dropped my bitch at the door, drew my service weapon (a Glock 22 .40 caliber pistol) and entered the residence with them.

Evidently someone had tipped off the suspect being that the house was empty. The only thing left behind was worn furniture. It was a trap house similar to the one I frequented in my adolescent years. We were certain no one ever lived in this dwelling. It was used for the purpose of cooking, storing, and selling drugs.

Serving search and arrest warrants with the narcotics officers was like being on a set of a motion picture, except it was real. I had one incident when we were executing an arrest warrant where I had to dive into the shower with a naked male suspect an order to handcuff him. I got soaking wet. That incident was the topic of discussion for a while amongst other officers. Let's just say, it took a while to live that one down.

Self-Value

In December of 2007, I earned my bachelor's Degree. I considered it a huge accomplishment, considering most of my grade school teachers thought I wouldn't even graduate high school. Some believed I wouldn't make it out of middle school. Ms. Gamble, one of my middle school teachers, knocked on my head with her knuckles as one would knock on a door.

"Knock, knock, is anyone here? Is anyone home?" she said, taunting me because of a question I answered incorrectly. I'm sure she didn't have a clue that she was watering the seed of low self-esteem and depression. The seed the Condescending Five had planted in the garden of my mind, body, and soul. There's not a farmer who could be as efficient as they were.

Unlike my High School graduation, my best friend, my sister in Christ, my mother attended. She cheered her "baby" on as I walked across the stage. In February of the following year, I moved to Miami Springs, Florida because my son lived there, and my daughter was only a five hour drive away.

After several months of unemployment, I was offered a position at Dade Juvenile Detention. I worked there as a Juvenile Detention Officer, but I functioned more like a counselor. After numerous failed attempts of my son's mother trying to rekindle old flames, she became upset and told me she was putting me on child support. I picked up a second job as a substitute teacher to help compensate for the high rate of child support (just below 40 percent) I was paying for two kids. I had been paying child support for both of my children previously, but it was based on agreements arranged with their mothers.

I enjoyed immensely, working with the juveniles incarcerated at Dade Juvenile Detention. I labored countless hours to meet their needs and earn their respect. I counseled and interacted with many residents. Nearly all of them had very interesting stories. Several of them were incarcerated for murder, attempted murder, conspiracy to commit murder, rape, armed robbery and other violent crimes. The majority of them were gang members. Some were Bloods, Cripps, MS13's, while others belonged to local gangs.

I spent a year and a half working with the residents of Dade Juvenile Detention. During one of my daily group discussions with about fifteen residents, I asked them how and why they became gang members. I also questioned why they embraced the street life and their hopes for the future. The answers I received caused my concern for their safety to heighten. It was like looking into my own eyes as a teen and asking those questions.

"Sir, what do you mean? Why did I join the MS13's? That's my family and no one else care for me. I sell crack, Sir, rob and steal so I can feed my son and baby momma. The reason I became violent is because, if you be nice, people will take advantage of you. Only the strong survive out here in the street."

I argued sharp and swift as they responded. "Family, huh? Really, so can you explain why you are sitting here and your family never visits you? You back there, are you the one who said only the strong survive? Can you show me the strength of the gangsters responsible for killing innocent women, kids, and men?"

I lectured the residents on the concept of self-value and how I came to understand it. I shared my testimony with them and instantly won their admiration.

"We like you, Sir. You are one of us. You can understand us. But sometimes 'you are too hard on us, though." Laughter and a few chuckles followed. I smiled and said, 'Yeah, but that's only because I care so much about all of you."

I loved those group sessions. Many staff were assaulted, threatened and attacked often. Somehow, I was never terrorized. Some would call it luck, but I'd like to call it respect. Some of the residents hoped for a better life. Others eagerly conversed with their family, attempting to secure a place to live when they were released. Otherwise they would be homeless. Some residents fought staff so they wouldn't get released, much like the homeless people I dealt with as a police officer. They would commit misdemeanor crimes during the winter months to get off the street, receive shelter, and three hot meals. It's quite unfortunate the reality those young kids were faced with, but that's the story of America's inner-city youth. I can only hope, in the end, after all of my redirection, counseling, testimony and fiery sermons about doing right, that I planted the seed of perseverance and self-value in at least one of them.

I resigned from the detention center in February of 2010. It was hard leaving those kids behind, but I moved forward with hopes of meeting them again. It was also disheartening knowing that the work I could do there was limited to what the policies and procedures dictated. I left hoping to launch my public speaking career. Although I was unsuccessful in my efforts to get established as a professional public speaker, I discovered the beautiful kids of Malcolm X Learning Center.

Malcolm X Learning Center is a public school located in south Miami Springs that serves Pre-k through fifth grade. About 97 percent of the 484 students there were classified as "economically disadvantaged", and 95 percent paid reduced lunch prices. It all happened when I was passing out some brochures promoting myself as a public speaker. I met Principal Green and his staff. They seemed to care deeply about the overall well-being and success of their students. The principal was straightforward and uncanny when he said, "Brandon, I like you and we need a man like you around, but the school budget just can't afford to compensate you for your services. You are welcome to speak to the kids if you are still interested."

"Absolutely, I will speak to them at no cost. I don't care much about being paid; I just want to get a start at doing what I love."

The principal smiled and said, "Well then, let's get started."

I didn't expect to give a speech, nor was I prepared when the principal marched me into a classroom full of students. He introduced me to the students and they formed a circle around me. After speaking with the kids, the principal walked over and shook my hand. He thanked me, gave me a tour of the school, and introduced me to his staff. He made copies of the brochure I handed him. The students wanted one and some of the staff did, too. I didn't expect to receive this sort of response and appreciation from the principal, staff, or students. I was moved by their generosity and warmth.

I lectured on the causes and effects of academic success and failure, explaining how their performance in school will impact their lives long after school. That speech developed into a series of speeches and lectures. I spoke there for the remainder of the school year, teaching from a variety of focus points with the primary focus on commitment to change, self-value, and testimony. I developed a team of dedicated and passionate people like myself to assist with mentoring and lecturing the students. The message I conveyed to the teachers helped them to better understand why some students behaved poorly. This also motivated the teachers to be more sincere in their efforts to ensure that each student is learning.

The essential tools I employed to motivate the students were relevant in and out of the classroom. Resulting from these efforts we saw increased test scores, perfect attendance from students who previously didn't, and enriched teacher-student relationships. Today, many of the challenges educators are faced with in the classroom are problems extending from students' personal lives.

Let's examine a story about a student at Malcolm X that had poor grades and attendance. All of the teachers dreaded having this student in their classes. He was very disruptive. The underlying story about this ten-year-old kid was that he spent most of his nights and early mornings alone at home. His mother was in the street smoking crack and prostituting. The kid didn't know his father because his father had been in prison since he was born. So this situation left the boy responsible for getting his two younger siblings ready for school, along with himself. After hearing the full story, it was easy to see that this child was a champion and my hero. After all of the disadvantages he endured outside of school, he still managed to attend. Although his attendance wasn't consistent, he deserved credit because he was sending himself to school. No one made him. He wasn't a kid, he was a ten-year-old man. He took responsibility for himself and his two younger siblings. This boy wasn't only an outstanding student, but an exceptionally underprivileged kid who evidently valued himself.

Another student there belonged to a local gang. It was said that he broke another kid's leg after the child refused to join his gang. The kid was in the fourth grade. He was only 9 years old.

One of the biggest compliments I received from a student at Malcolm X was when a kid interrupted a speech I was giving to ask me about becoming a public speaker. He said he would like to talk to kids and help people like I was doing. He asked me towards the end of our "Q and A", "Do people have to look like that to become a speaker?"

"Like what?" I asked him curiously.

"Like the hair around your mouth and wear nice clothes like you're wearing."

I realized he was complimenting my appearance. With a huge grin, I thanked him. "Not at all little guy. I'm sure when you start speaking; you'll look more handsome than me." He smiled as I moved on to engage other enthusiastic students competing for my attention. I will never forget Malcolm X and the lovely students there. I'm looking forward to returning someday to follow up with the students. I found that helping and encouraging them helped me as much as it helped them. I was able to mend old wounds I didn't realize still existed from the abuse I suffered earlier in life. The remarks of the boy who implied I was handsome served as therapy for me. He helped build my confidence. Madea had always reminded me of how ugly and dark I am, or how big my head is. I was often described by Madea as a "big black ugly gorilla". So I guess, in my subconscious, I still kind of believed that. I still struggle with insecurities today spanning further than physical appearance.

Every day I'm growing stronger, continually healing and regenerating the pillars of self-value that were destroyed by years of abuse. The late Tupac Shakur defined the acronym 'THUG LIFE' tattooed on his abdomen as "The Hate U Give Little Infants Fucks Everyone". I remain loving and caring despite the hate I received as a child.

Parting ways with the students of Malcolm X was even harder than leaving Dade Juvenile Detention. To walk away from so many innocent faces that depended on me was one of the hardest things I've done. I left the school because I was relocating back to Tennessee to marry a woman I had a crush on since my senior year of college.

A dream come true is the way I felt when my longtime friend Denise Hardy flew from Los Angeles to Miami Springs to visit me. Words couldn't describe my emotions and feelings of blissfulness. I worked extra hours so that I could take her around the city and have a great time. I didn't have a living room set, so I went out and purchased a cheap one. I cleaned my apartment spotless and bought an Egyptian cotton comforter set for my bed. The comforter was her favorite colors: Sunset orange and North Carolina blue.

Just before her plane landed, I was in the airport parking lot hammering out a few sets of pushups. I wiped away the sweat from my forehead as I entered the airport to await her arrival. The Los Angeles flight landed and passengers were walking in the direction of the luggage claim area. I scanned the crowd anxiously, my heart fluttering while I tried to keep my cool. There, walking behind the Hispanic woman, I saw lengthy hair and big, pretty eyes. Denise! She walked smoothly, and her hair bounced with each stride, as well as other blessed parts of her body. The light brown complexion of this Caribbean beauty was flawless. I spotted her before she saw me. I tried to catch up to her to whisper in her ear but she quickly turned the corner and entered the ladies room.

When she came out, I said, "Hey lady, how have you been? It's been a long time. You look nice." I extended my arm to hand her the bouquet of sunset orange roses. If I could've found Carolina blue roses, I would've bought those, too. She reached for the roses, lost balance and fell into my arms. It turned out; she was aiming to impress me, too, by wearing the high heels that nearly caused her to fall.

I escorted her to my car, which was over-saturated with the strawberry air freshener I sprayed moments earlier. I pretended not to smell it when Denise said, "Wow, your car smells good." The truth was, gym towels and wet swimming trunks were what my car normally smelled like.

I placed her luggage in my trunk and drove out of the MIA Airport parking lot. I was so preoccupied with chatting and staring at this lovely Afro-Bahamian beauty, I actually got lost.

"Are you going in circles?" she asked.

"Oh no, I got it. It's just around the corner."

After a few more wrong turns, I admitted to her that I was lost. We eventually made it back to my apartment nearly an hour and a half later; a drive that should've been twenty-five minutes or less. This would serve as an occasional joke she would refer to later on.

I introduced her to my roommate when we walked in.

"Damn, you are pretty! What you doing with this boy?" he said jokingly.

The three of us talked for a while and discussed plans for the night. Denise, exhausted from her flight and working the previous night, went into my bedroom and fell fast asleep. After the sleeping beauty awakened, I treated her to one of the finest restaurants in Miami. Chef

José Andrés's world-renowned restaurant, The Bazaar, is located in South Beach's SLS Hotel.

We pulled up in front of the hotel and were received by a valet. My broke butt never parked valet, especially with all the child support I was paying. But I was trying hard to impress this woman. And it paid off. Denise surprised me with our first kiss as we entered the restaurant.

We laughed hard, dined well, and caught up on old times. Brian joined us thirty minutes later and commented on how nice the view was. He started talking to a woman sitting next to us. They spoke as if they had known one another for a long time. I guess a little alcohol and a bit of charm has that effect on most of us. We laughed at Brian most of the night. He is a true comedian and friend.

When we left The Bazaar, we waited outside and chatted until the valet brought my car out front and handed over the keys. I thank him and we got in. The valet standing at my door smiled until I drove away.

"Wow, Denise, I guess that's the kind of treatment people get here. Did you see that valet?"

"Yeah, I did. I think he was waiting for his tip," she replied with a sexy Caribbean accent.

"A tip, are you serious? He was waiting for a tip? He better tip out of my face. That place is costly enough," I remarked.

We hung out and enjoyed ourselves the entire weekend before she departed for Los Angeles. I took Denise on a limited shopping spree. I called it limited because she was limited to purchasing mostly sales items from JC Penney and Gap. Denise boarded her flight donning the skinny jeans and a multicolored sweater I bought her at Gap.

"Damn, that ass looks good in those jeans," I mumbled to myself. "Too bad I've been practicing abstinence for the past two and a half years."

I called her hours later to make sure she made it back to Los Angeles safely. We continued to chat most of the day and night over the phone, via email, and text. We just couldn't get enough of each other.

Several months later, Denise decided to return to CSU to pursue a doctoral degree in education, and I agreed to move back to Tennessee to be with her. I moved to Midland in the summer of 2010. Denise moved in with me a few months later. And the romance was ignited. We started making plans for marriage. We didn't have money for a big wedding, so we married in a small church in Davis. Soon after, we discussed relocating because CSU had cut her scholarship. The university was rumored to be battling with their usual budget problems and misappropriated funds. The only reason either of us considered moving back to Midland was for the scholarship, anyway. My wife's family began to openly express their discontentment towards me, citing how Denise shouldn't have married me especially since I was a cop. They believed policemen were generally violent and abusive to their spouses. My wife's family hated me, though I hadn't yet had the opportunity to meet them.

We moved to Northbrook, Illinois in July of 2011, a suburb located thirty minutes north of Chicago. It took a while to get readjusted to working in the prison system again. I was working at Chicago Correctional Institution (CCI). The facility had multiple units that contained two circular levels where they housed the inmates. Each level had thirty inmates. The bottom level also included a common area. This is where the inmates from both levels congregated. Their common area had a large screen television. It had tables for card games, microwave ovens, a sitting area, and two telephones. The common area looked pretty much like a street corner where a gathering of dealers and users took place.

In fact, many of the inmates bought, sold, and used drugs. Some of the high profile inmates would arrange the purchase of cell phones between inmates and officers. They paid staff to smuggle in cell phones, drugs, food and other contraband. At that time, the going rate for any cell phone was five-hundred dollars. That easily enticed dirty correctional officers. Many of the inmates that controlled the facility had sex with some of the female officers. It was a fair exchange; it appeared the female officers willfully engaged without being paid to.

With their cell phones, inmates accomplished small things, like checking and posting pictures to their Facebook page, to large things, like ordering hits on people in or out of prison.

Their operation was well organized. The assistance of corrupt correctional officers made it hard to catch them. Throughout my entire career working as a public servant, I've met a lot of interesting people. I encountered quite a few gang members and held long conversations and interviews with most of them. Among the gangs there were the Gangster Disciples (GD), Vice Lords, MS13's, Cripps, and Bloods. The gang members echoed the same thoughts as the residents of Dade Juvenile Detention when questioned. "Blood in, blood out", "This isn't a gang, its family", "Its protection. It's a way of life," most of them would tell me. There were many inmates there that took a strong liking to me.

Some of them even challenged other inmates when they became aggressive or used abusive language towards me. "Hey man what you doing fucking with Tennessee, he cool people. Alright, when that big country mother fucker come over here and knock your ass out, don't be saying shit then nigga." I was proactive at CCI and became very popular rather quickly with staff and inmates alike. However, I also inherited my share of people that disliked me and some who even threatened to take my life. I've had threats made on my life since my early childhood and while serving as a police officer. I experienced the same threatening language when I worked in juvenile and adult mental health facilities. I, like Apostle Paul, have been in danger in the city and in the field.

Conversely, this time was different. I had a wife. I didn't view threats on my life the way I had before. I stopped brushing them off and began to realize that having my life taken was a real possibility. There were rumors that some of the staff within Illinois State Department of Corrections, particularly CCI, were active gang members. This made it difficult to trust my coworkers.

I wrote an inmate an infraction for threatening another inmate. The inmate was due for a parole hearing. The infraction he received for making threats would substantially decrease his chances of being released. I wasn't aware that he was due for a hearing and judging from his aggressive behavior he wasn't, either. Normally, whenever inmates were due for a hearing they were always on their best behavior, unless they didn't want to be released. This actually happens in some cases.

After the inmate received the infraction, he told me, "I'm gonna fuck you up nigga. I know what you drive, bitch," and he gestured in the air in either a punching or stabbing motion. This inmate was a known Blood gang member. According to departmental policy, when an incident like this occurs, the inmate would be removed from "general population" and separated from the officer he has targeted. The inmate would be placed on twenty-three hour lock-down. His cell would be searched for weapons and other contraband. An investigation would ensue to gather information on the inmate and his activity.

None of this happened. I was met with defiance from my official who chose to deviate from policy for questionable reasons. He didn't separate the inmate from me, nor did he place him on lock-down. Some of the senior correctional officers told me to leave for the day and say I was sick. I chose not to leave and continued working in the same area as the inmate.

Officers got attacked at correctional facilities daily, sometimes killed. One officer was beaten so severely, he was released from CCI on a medical retirement. It was reported that several other officers were present during the attack and stood watch. They watched as a fellow correctional officer got subdued by an inmate and nearly beaten to death. This event occurred during my first week on the job. That is a mild example of the risk correctional officers take when they are locked behind bars in penal institutions with some of the worst people society has produced.

The slaying of a celebrated correctional officer and the conspiracies regarding his murder caused me a great deal of distress. The fact that I was a former police officer working in a prison made me paranoid. One of the inmates might have tried to make a name for themselves if they learned this. I had credible threats made on my life. I resigned from CCI because I felt I couldn't trust some of the officers and officials.

by Brandon Williams

After leaving CCI, I took on a position with the Center for Youth, a non-profit residential treatment center that served DJS (Department of Juvenile Services) and DSS (Department of Social Services) juveniles. Most of the residents suffered from behavioral disorders or mental illnesses.

The majority of the population at Center for Youth was female. The campus had eight dormitory-style buildings which housed the residents. I was part of the Behavior Intervention team, assisting the residents having emotional or behavioral problems. Whenever the residents had a crisis, they were usually very animated and violent. I understood why; that's how they were accustomed to expressing their frustration. The angels of Center for Youth, as some often called them, were awesome whenever they weren't kicking, screaming, punching, spitting or throwing things at the staff.

I fell in love with all of the residents, and every one of them had a touching story. I developed close bonds and encouraged all of them to strive for the best in life. Many of my female residents were victims of rape and prostitution. Some were also mothers. The residents were between the ages of thirteen and seventeen. Many of them abused drugs and dealt with conflicts that the average adult cannot understand or cope with.

Among the mountain of stories, little "Janice" stands out. She was in her early teens when she was raped repeatedly by a relative. Janice then told her mother, who ignored and scolded her for telling her. She was ignored by her family and no one came to her aid. With no one to turn to for help, she turned to the street, the only option made available to her. However, the street was not safe, either.

She talked about the time she was dragged into the bushes and raped by an adult male. She also started prostituting to earn money to buy food and school supplies. This reflects the rationale of my younger self when I was dealing crack. Soon after, Janice started selling her body to men and hiring herself out to women. She never intended on sleeping with women, but noted that more women than men approached her for sex. Janice reluctantly accepted female clients so she would not lose the potential earnings. By this time, she had already conceived a child, adding more responsibility.

She loved to write about her past, as well as her daily life. That was a sort of escape for her; it made her happy.

"Mr. Williams, would you like to read some of my writings?" I sat and read with her almost every day. She was my inspiration to write. I struggled with writing about my past because it hurt. It was depressing for me. So how did she find peace in writing? Little Janice told me to keep writing my story and not give up. She asked me for a copy of my book once I completed it. At the time, I had less than a twenty thousand word manuscript.

by Brandon Williams

Another dilemma was that I couldn't type. But, I could text faster than the average teen. I completed my manuscript by typing it into a free trial version of a Documents To Go application on my cell phone. The free trial came with my outdated, beaten-up Blackberry 8030 smartphone I purchased years earlier.

People rarely take the time to understand why people behave the way they do. Because of this, many of us will never come to know the stories of people like little Janice.

A resident once gave me a fake $10,000 check for my "excellent service". I was happy until I realized that she had given one to another staff member. I became jealous, but she encouraged me not to be. She felt we were excellent staff members, and both of us deserved a reward. I was once nominated for Employee of the Month by my supervisor, but lost to a senior staff. The loss didn't bother me because I had my fake check, and that meant more.

Unfortunately, my work with Center for Youth was short-lived when I took on a new job in New York, which paid fifteen thousand dollars more than what I was currently making. If I could have afforded to stay, I would have.

One night at work, I found myself on the corner of Broadway and Seventh Ave, New York's Times Square. A homeless man was searching through the trash for food. He reminded me of my childhood years, and represented what my life could've been like today.

He was rummaging through the trash systematically, hoping to find his next meal. I stood at a distance and watched him quietly. I searched for something meaningful to say, words that would change the course of his life. But those priceless words laid undiscovered within the cloud of confusion that enveloped me.

"Williams, it's time to go! We got a suspicious package call." Items reported as suspicious packages may pose a possible threat to life or property. They can contain explosives, chemicals, and biological agents. With heightened sensitivity in the wake of the Boston Marathon bombings, we handled every suspicious package report like the real thing until determined otherwise by members of the Explosive Ordnance Disposal unit (EOD). I got into my cruiser, initiated my overhead emergency lights and sirens, and drove away. Within a year, I returned to Midland, where I co-own a small but successful shipping company. In addition to this, my days are normally spent running a non-profit, 501 (c) (3), organization I founded. Our mission is to raise awareness and reduce domestic violence, juvenile delinquency and promote healthy living. It is profoundly amazing where life can bring us when we are truly in search of ourselves.

Some of the terms have been altered to protect the interest of some of the individuals mentioned within my story. If you enjoyed and embraced my story, then the following appeal is for you. I petition you to write a review of my (our) book and post it on websites you frequent.

by Brandon Williams

This is more than a call to action, it is the onset of a national movement for empowerment and awareness. But without your help there will be no movement. Therefore, I petition you to get at least one person to purchase our book. In turn that person must inspire someone to purchase this book as well. It is my hope that in the coming months we would have sold hundreds of thousands of copies of our book.

This will bring substantial attention to the various topics revealed within our story. It would also establish and validate me as an authority on those topics. Subsequently, giving a voice to the voiceless. I will speak for our cause and those who identify with our story. There is power in unity and together we will succeed.

"THE END"

Poems

THE FLOWER YOU DON'T SEE

I am like the flower you don't see. The one that takes more time than

the rest for you to see its beauty The one that grows deep into the

earth's floor

So it could bare its beauty much longer than the rest

But who has the wisdom or the patience

To take pride in a flower like me It's easier to pick the first thing you

see

The one that blossoms quickly and dies fast

Preserve yourself for me the flower you don't see.

by Brandon Williams

CHANGE

I resolve to evolve in the face of terror

My present state is getting weary; my heart is overripe with sorrow

I bow my head and pray to God for a better tomorrow

Yesterday's torment has past

Today springs hope for a brighter tomorrow

Who is fearless and is not weak in the face of victory's defeat

Earth conquered its conquest, putting our souls to rest

Some prevail but many fail, fail to die to self

We need not remain, I encourage you to change

Change as I speak, change as you weep!

You are my founders' feet, we are one in the same

Destiny is within us, promise is in us

The future is clear when change is here

I am not the same, I change evermore

You look me over with care and dare to say I remain

I may appear the same outwardly

And sound the same when you talk to me

But that don't justify your placing doubt in me

Even in the presence of fear

I am forever in search of promise, the promise inside of me

I am not the same, I've changed!

UNSURE

I am unsure where life will lead me when I am released from this jail

I am unsure of the people that claim to love me

I am unsure of the man I love and his feeling for me

I am unsure where I will sleep every night but Lord

One thing that I am sure of is you JESUS, and your love for me and

all mankind

I am sure that if I stay with you, I will be filled with love and peace

-Jackie Williams

36199587R00196

Made in the USA
Middletown, DE
12 February 2019